GARBAGE BAG SUITCASE
A Memoir

BY SHENANDOAH CHEFALO

MISSION POINT PRESS

Published by Mission Point Press

Library of Congress Control Number:
2016901837

Readers are encouraged to go to
www.MissionPointPress.com to contact
the author or to find information on how to
buy this book in bulk at a discounted rate.

Published by Mission Point Press
2554 Chandler Lake Rd.
Traverse City, MI 49686
(231) 421-9513
www.MissionPointPress.com

ISBN: 978-1-943995-03-5

Printed in the United States of America.

This story is mine, but it is for the millions of independents—those children who are alone, no guidance, no voice . . . and fading hope.

CONTENTS

INTRODUCTION

Several years ago, I became unsettled in my career, and started searching for ways to take the myriad of skills I had learned and transition them into something new.

While traveling, I listened to Jack Canfield's *The Success Principles*, and something about coaching kept sticking out. I wasn't sure at the time what coaching was, but one Google search later I had signed myself up for a week-long intensive coaching program in Atlanta, Georgia. On the plane down I was nervous, having absolutely no idea what to expect, yet completely thrilled and entranced with the idea.

During the coaching classes, I worked through my own personal development program to help me better understand what the process would be like when I became a coach. The process required improving myself through such areas as increasing consciousness, building wealth, enhancing skills and assessing my values, needs and goals as they related to my personal foundation. This involved facing issues from my past that I had long ago decided never need be discussed, or even thought about. Things I thought belonged locked away in a closet, where all skeletons are kept.

Throughout the class I was good at putting on my game face, getting through the situation while revealing as little about myself as possible. Over the years, I had become proficient in giving minimal details about myself, and most people knew very little about me. I wasn't withdrawn or shy, I had learned to talk but express or reveal little. Even after I started on the journey of writing this book, when I mentioned my experience in foster care most people who asked what the book was about were stunned.

Once back home from my classes, I busied myself with preparing to launch my new coaching company. As in most of my previous jobs and businesses, I was good at pouring myself into the start-up phases, and pushing the rest to the side. The classes had revealed many of my personal weaknesses, but as I had done through my life, I thought

GARBAGE BAG SUITCASE

ignoring the negatives and burying myself in work would make the issues go away.

I began working on my company website. It was a struggle, trying to figure out my target audience, trying to write text that would captivate and intrigue possible clients. I struggled most with the "About Me" section. How could I write something compelling about myself? I hadn't accomplished anything of significance, and I had spent a lifetime trying to be average. Now I needed to actively stand out and set myself apart from the crowd. I required copy that would make people want to hire me. I needed words that made me seem special.

Reaching out through my extensive business network, I was introduced to a gentleman who was once a newspaper reporter, now working in private industry. I explained my dilemma. He completely understood, and suggested that he interview me as he used to interview famous people in the past. From this interview he would write an article that could be used as the biographical information for my website.

It sounded like a great idea, and we agreed to meet the following day. We had originally planned for a one-hour meeting, but almost three hours later, it was clear that the interview was turning into something more. Soon, he and I were conversing about more than just my accomplishments. He was diving into my personal life details, details that I had shared with very few people. It started with a question that I received a lot in my life: "Shenandoah, how did you get that name?" As I began to tell him the story about how I got my name, or at least the story that I had been told about it, he became more intrigued.

"Have you ever thought about writing a book?"

It seems like yesterday when he asked me that seemingly simple question, yet it was nearly four years ago. "No, I don't think I'm a writer, and anyway, who would want to read about me?" I answered, trying to defer the conversation. It was a tactic in which I had become quite skilled.

By the end of our marathon interview session, he promised to have a piece to me by the end of the week, and he did. I loved the article he wrote about me, and put it up on my website immediately. But he wouldn't let the idea about the book go. After several emails, he had convinced me to sit down and write a few pages. He promised that he would look them over and let me know what he honestly thought.

So I did. I sat down and typed out nearly thirty pages without much thought. The pages included random stories, descriptions of memories that seemed interesting. Nothing life changing; or so I thought. I shipped them off to him. Under two hours later I got an email asking when I could have more pages done. He wanted to know what happened next. I couldn't believe it. *What was so interesting about this story?* I wasn't even sure what else I could say, and told him so.

He responded that what he found so interesting was this dichotomy he perceived in me. He knew me from my work in the community, things other professionals had said about me, and the transition I had told him about from my professional work into this new idea of coaching. Then there were these thirty pages of text, discussing and detailing my nomadic upbringing. How could that kind of childhood lead to this successful person here today? He couldn't reconcile the contrast.

I had never really thought about my childhood from this perspective. I never viewed myself as successful, and I never believed I had accomplished much of anything. In fact, I was (am) still trying to figure out my talent. I started thinking about my personal development classes and about the readings I had been doing on the law of attraction and other self-help areas. I thought about the hundreds of legal clients that had been into our office, lamenting about their situations. Questions began swirling around in my mind, and I became consumed. I began researching foster care statistics and alumni statistics. I was reading every article I could find about foster care outcomes, aging out of the system and the general process of foster care. I suddenly came face-to-face with the truth in a way I never had.

Without much work, I soon discovered that less than 1% of foster children receive a four-year degree, and that out of the nearly 1.6 million people incarcerated in the various correctional institutions nationwide, 1.3 million had been in the foster care system, or 80%. I knew that the system wasn't great and I knew that I had struggled, but I had never taken the time to understand how bad it was. Over 400,000 children in foster care are affected every year and the number is growing.

In care, I always felt isolated and alone. It was a familiar feeling for me, and truthfully I thought it was how everyone felt. It never occurred to me how many others experienced the same pain. As soon as I understood that the suffering I felt as a child was being felt by millions of other children, I knew that it was time for a new solution. I needed to share my story.

In the years of research I've conducted for this book, I learned the general population does not understand the impact that the foster care system has on a person, and the lasting marks that it makes on our communities. It is often unclear what happens after the children are removed from their homes, or what happens after these children turn 18.

This book, and especially Part Two, is meant to be an honest and open discussion about areas that make foster children view the world a little differently. It is also the part of the book where I talk openly about possible solutions, things that can be done in a very real way to make the impact of foster care less disruptive in a child's life. These outcomes can be far more positive for the children and their communities. While there are many great organizations working to solve this problem, I in no way believe that the solutions I present are the only answers. What I do know is that if we do not come together to solve this problem, we will continue to have millions of children, now adults, who have never known love, safety or stability.

This story is mine, but I tell it for the millions of independents, those children who are alone, with no guidance, with no voice. Together, we will change this system!

PART ONE: WHAT IS NORMAL?

CHAPTER ONE
OH! SHENANDOAH

*"The best way to not get your heart broken is pretend
you don't have one." —Charlie Sheen*

I WAS ALONE IN THE HOUSE.

I was four.

Along one side of my small bedroom was a homemade bookshelf, made of concrete blocks and two-by-fours. My stuffed animals sat inside, arranged by size. They had become my only friends.

Little me with my stringy blonde curls, dressed in hand-me-downs collected from various charity organizations and garage sales. I hunkered down for my favorite time of the day, when Bill Cosby's "Picture Pages" came on in the middle of Captain Kangaroo, teaching basic math, geometry and drawing. I would dance to the song and await the arrival of the lesson, complete with silly characters like Mortimer Ichabod Marker. Oh, how I longed for my very own Mortimer Ichabod Marker pen, perhaps as much as Ralphie from "A Christmas Story" longed for his Red Ryder B.B. gun.

The contagious theme song would stick in my head all day. *"Picture Pages, Picture Pages, Time to get your picture pages, time to get your crayons and your pencils. Picture Pages, Picture Pages, Open up your picture pages. Time to watch Bill Cosby do a picture page with you."*

Being alone, and inside, was normal. I felt safest when I was locked inside my room, protected from the elements, protected from people and isolated. It certainly was far safer than being with my mom, any of her friends, or the endless string of boyfriends we lived with. It was especially safer than being with my dad. The outside was an unknown, and other kids were intimidating and difficult for me to navigate.

One day, on the advice of another television great, Mister Rogers, I decided to push my beloved stuffed friends in a carriage to the park, both to take them on an adventure and to get a much-needed reprieve from the yelling inside. There was no escaping the random violence of my childhood. As I stepped outside, I could see that most of the houses, including ours, had dust for yards and there were no trees. There was no grass in sight, just a single cactus. Across the street, the neighbors had decided their yard was a good place to work on a broken down old car. It appeared that progress was slow, because that old car remained on blocks for the entire three weeks that we had lived there.

As I prepared to leave, I neatly arranged my stuffed friends in the old carriage with my favorite, Love Bunny, having the best seat. Then in order of fondness I placed the walrus, monkey and my tattered old lion securely in the back.

The tires on the carriage wobbled as I timidly made my way down the maze of dusty concrete. There wasn't much to see. Gray cement in every direction; a few feet away a single yellow dandelion pushed through the hardened landscape, the only color in sight. I had made it several blocks, before I noticed a group of children, older than me, maybe aged ten or twelve. They were kicking a stone down the sidewalk, laughing and teasing one another. It wasn't long before the sole boy in the group noticed me. He hit the girl to his left on the shoulder and began to point in my direction. Quickly, the ragtag group of kids surrounded me. The boy reached into my carriage without warning and ripped my friends away from me. He tossed the stuffed animals to the other kids. Laughs and howling ensued, quickly turning into taunts and provocation.

One girl seemed to quickly regret her actions, perhaps noticing the tears streaming down my face, as she tried to cajole the others into returning the stuffed animals. It took some time, but eventually she was successful. All of the animals were returned to the carriage, but it was too late. I was defeated. I began making my way back home. Running. Barely able to keep up with the carriage, which was now going down hill. I could hear the older kids as they seemed close behind. Quickly, I retreated into our trailer, careful not to slam the door. From inside I heard the shouts, taunts and jeers of the kids as they passed by.

I disappeared into my small bedroom unnoticed by those around me. I felt so alone and violated that I vowed to never go outside again. Unable or unwilling to risk any more, I found solace in my picture books and my stuffed animal friends, including my best friend, Love Bunny.

Our family never stayed in one place very long, months, weeks, sometimes even days, then often leaving suddenly and without notice. One of the toughest parts of constantly moving and meeting new kids was telling them my name - Shenandoah - and being asked to explain why I had such a weird name. At a young age I began telling people one of the few things that I thought I could remember about who I was and where I came from: "I'm named after the Shenandoah Hotel in Las Vegas. I think it's where my parents met. At least it wasn't the Tropicana." This answer typically led to chuckles, and the conversation would usually move on to something else. It was a story I'd heard my father tell on numerous occasions, and I had adopted it as my own.

It wasn't until 30 years later that I learned I wasn't named after the Shenandoah Hotel in Las Vegas. The hotel didn't even open until May of 1980, nearly five years after I was born. And though I thought I had memories of sitting at the bar drinking Shirley Temples while my parents gambled, I now know the story my father told was a lie, a lie to cover for other lies.

My world was one of deception, half-truths, and escape. Escape from landlords looking for past-due rent, escape from entanglements, lovers, fights, neighbors. Escape from the unknown. Whenever somebody began to cast a judging eye, we hastily picked up what little we had and headed for the next place. My belongings whittled down to little or nothing. I stuffed them into a tattered garbage bag that I came to know as my suitcase.

I thought everybody lived this way. Surely the sitcom families I saw on TV, with their attentive parents and well-kept homes, were not based on real life. They were obviously based on the way people wished it could be, right? My parents fought, yelled and screamed and threw stuff at each other. My mother once hurled a pair of nail clippers at my father, missing his head by mere inches, but with so much force and velocity that the clippers lodged in the door frame of one of our many rental houses. I don't recall what the fight was about, but the clippers remained there; a silent reminder until we escaped in the middle of the night months later. I was given no explanation when my mother woke me from sleep, tapping me on the shoulder. "Ten minutes to gather all your stuff; we have to go," she said in a whisper.

I was groggy, and grabbed only Love Bunny. All of my other neatly arranged stuffed animals, clothes, and books were left behind. My mother and I drove for hours without stopping. The darkness stretched in all directions, my eyes heavy staring at the white line in the road. A lampshade rubbed against my face the entire time. "Are we there yet?" I asked, tired and cranky. As with most of our evacuations my father wasn't with us, though he always seemed to reappear again a few days or weeks later.

It seemed perfectly rational that my parents got that mad at each other in front of me. They drank until they couldn't stand, and sniffed and smoked and took pills in front of me, which would always make them act weird. Sometimes they would laugh uncontrollably, other times they would get angry at the smallest of things. They slept late, missed going to their jobs, and often forgot to go to the grocery store, leaving us with little food in the house. They rarely asked about school or homework, and seldom did they know where I was.

We had arrived one more time in a new town, a new home. Here I was alone in the house, again. This time, it was a small place tucked on a corner lot, a graveyard just beyond the view of the living room window. I lay on the floor in a small bedroom. Curled in the corner. Nervous, worried and scared. Love Bunny's head was soaked in my tears, waiting to be rescued, waiting to be noticed.

CHAPTER TWO
ACCIDENTS HAPPEN

"I don't believe in accidents. There are only
encounters in history. There are no accidents."
—Pablo Picasso

THE LOG CABIN INN was somewhere in Colorado. A small tavern, built of faux logs that stood in the parking lot of a strip mall. The doors were heavy, and as we stepped inside the large room was filled with cigarette smoke that circled and lingered just below the lights over each table. A blinking Pabst Blue Ribbon sign and a frayed and stained Denver Broncos flag hung behind the bar.

My father and his team had just finished a softball tournament and were celebrating at the sponsor's place of business. I had grown up in bars, just like this one, and had gotten pretty good at occupying myself playing pool or arcade games. We had been there several hours, and I was getting restless. My father, annoyed that I was sitting at the table listening in to the adult conversation, decided it was time to go. As my dad stumbled out to his small pick-up truck, I eagerly jumped up onto the bench seat. I was excited to be going home, out of the dark and smelly bar.

"Want to play a game?" he asked, resting his head on the steering wheel while he fumbled to put his keys in the ignition.

"Yes!" I yelled, excited to be engaged in any activity that wasn't of my own making. "What do we do?" As we started to pull out of the parking lot and make our way toward the road, my father explained that I would need to tell him the color of each and every traffic light as we drove. I would get extra points if I could remember which way we needed to turn, left or right, to make our way back home. I was seven.

"This sounds like fun! I bet I can get way more points than you."

I really thought we were playing a game. Each time my father would approach a traffic light he would yell out the color of the light, and I would yell, "No, it's red, silly!" I was so small that I didn't know it mattered. The Red Light Game, as it became known, was played on far too many occasions.

Every stereotype that you could harbor about some men fit my dad. He was full of statistics about every sport, a master at trivia, and off-color jokes. He knew a lot of useless information, and used that to get people to trust and like him. He was everyman. He played softball for many teams and a big part of my life was going to see him play. He was small in stature — 5'7" — with long dark hair. Later when he cut his hair shorter, a rat-tail remained. He had a developing paunch resulting from a diet of fast food, alcohol and recreational drugs.

People seemed to not only tolerate him, but to enjoy his company. Perhaps, his best quality was his ability to blend into a group of people. I learned that skill from him, to not rock the boat, get along with everyone, never take a stance one way or another. Nobody was ever going to question him and no one ever did. He never disagreed in public, and always went with the flow. But when the front door closed, he turned into another person: controlling, argumentative, contentious and mean.

One of the many jobs my dad had was working as a janitor for the local police station. That was brazen for someone who was running from the police, and his ability to take this type of risk made me even more cautious of him. The officers at the station liked and appreciated him so much that when my mom called to say that he had beaten her after one of their typical drunken rages, causing a black eye that needed stitches, they laughed it off and didn't visit to press charges. I spent the night on a friend's couch. We moved three days later. My dad reappeared a few weeks later.

My dad worked mostly as a janitor early in my life, and later as a landscaper, first for others, then on his own. He mowed lawns, cleaned yards and fixed irrigation systems in the deserts of Nevada. When I wasn't left home alone with the TV as a babysitter I would go with him to work. I had various odd jobs that included pulling weeds, holding the trash bags (for which there is a right and a wrong way,) raking up leaves, and sweeping the grass trimmings from the driveways. I spent lots of time with him driving from job site to job site.

When it rained it was impossible to do the landscaping work and it was a reprieve from standing in the hot sun pulling weeds. Rain days were a blessing and a curse. Because we were living in the desert, the water was needed. But my dad's sense of humor got the best of him on these days. To celebrate, my dad would drive down the Las Vegas Strip, looking for unsuspecting tourists.

One day in the early 1980s he spotted a man wearing a white suit; white pants, white blazer and a pastel shirt showing underneath. He was the perfect target for my dad and his practical joke. My father noticed him from several blocks away, the streets were mostly empty as the rain continued to pour down. As the light turned green, Dad raced through the intersection and pulled into the far right lane, slowing slightly as timing was everything. Just as the man began walking toward us, my father sped through the puddle collecting between the road and the gutter. The water sprayed everywhere. As we passed the man my father was in tears from laughing. I turned to look behind us as the man stood screaming, his pristine white suit now covered in dirty roadside water. "That's what he gets for wearing a suit in the rain!" I chuckled, but felt sad all at once. My father continued to laugh and soon I joined in.

Once I was old enough to be in school full-time, I began working with my father every weekend and over the school and summer breaks. We seemed to always be together. Once, as he was attempting to repair a broken sprinkler head, he grew agitated. He called me to bring him a tool. Apparently I didn't move quickly enough. As I approached him with the tool, he grabbed my arm and threw me face down onto the ground. My face smashed into the lawn, leaving a gash in my forehead from bouncing off the sprinkler head. I became motionless, afraid to move and even more afraid to cry.

Prior "accidents" had taught me that tears, or the showing of any emotion, ensured further scorn and more pain. I inhaled sharply, choking back the tears, trying to figure out what I had done wrong and how I could avoid another calamity in the future. I spent much of my time trying to figure out how to avoid these mishaps, but it seemed I was always one step behind. My father later claimed to my mother that I'd fallen down. I was just uncoordinated, of course.

It seems I was a very clumsy child, between the number of sprinklers I fell on, the various door handles that I walked into, and the periodic staircases I tripped down. With my father it was always dangerous. He needed no provocation to unleash his rage.

On one hot Las Vegas day, the kind of day that fills your lungs with scorched dry desert air, my father and I were driving in his taxi-cab yellow 1970's Toyota Hilux with two bucket seats. No one, at least in my family, wore seat belts. We were traveling through a wealthy neighborhood, placing fliers in mailboxes, searching for new landscaping clients. If I stretched just enough, and perched myself on the armrest, I could see out the side window. The houses seemed extremely large and wonderful, and I remember daydreaming about who might live inside. *Kings and Queens*, I thought.

I peered out the window in thought, all my weight resting on the armrest. Then, as we rounded the corner, my father reached across me and pulled up on my door handle. The car door flung open. I fell out and rolled onto the asphalt road, coming to rest on someone's lawn. I laid there for an eternity, frozen with fear. Finally realizing I was uninjured, I remained still, and looked at the bright sky above. Tears welled in my eyes, not from physical pain, but from the pain I knew was about to be inflicted on me.

I heard footsteps and the wells turned to a full river, streaming down my face. I could have filled a bucket with all my tears. I knew I would be in trouble for falling from the car, and now from crying.

"Are you okay?" I heard. It was a delicate, feminine voice. I'd been expecting the growl of my father screaming at me for embarrassing him and opening the car door. Everything bad that happened was my fault, and he always gave me a detailed breakdown for why it was my fault. Instead I heard the softest, sweetest voice ask, "Little girl, are you okay?" I turned my head toward her voice and began to soften my sobbing. "Uh-huh?" I said, still unsure if I could or should move.

"Who were you in that car with?" she asked as she knelt down beside me. She was gorgeous. *A princess*, I thought. She had long blonde hair that brushed against my face as she helped me to a seated position.

"My daddy," I replied, as she carefully examined me to see if anything was broken.

"What happened?" she asked. I was staring at her green floral shift dress. It was so beautiful.

I'd been in this position before, many times before, whenever an outsider or teacher questioned me about a bruise, being late, or where my parents were. I learned through experience that answering these questions was not simple. The truth was never acceptable, and giving the wrong excuse or cover-up usually meant I would be on the receiving end of a very severe punishment.

"I don't know," I answered, meekly. Those words had become the perfect substitute for explanation. I already knew my father was going to blow a gasket, and there was no way I was adding additional punishment for speaking the truth. Like everything else in my life, it was a secret, and it would remain that way.

I could see she wasn't buying into my answers, but before she could speak I heard screeching tires and my father ranting before he even left the vehicle. I had been lying in the yard for over 10 minutes, and I'd been worried about where he had gone. *Did he plan on leaving me? And what if he did come back, what would he do when he found me?*

Being left behind had become a constant worry, because it was a constant threat. When we were packing my father would remind me frequently, "Children could be left behind if they didn't hurry quick enough." Like my toys and other belongings, I too could be left and forgotten about, waiting for someone else to claim me. I was tormented by this idea. I was afraid that if I didn't come home directly after school they might disappear, leaving me alone forever.

Maybe he would leave me this time? Surely this nice stranger would take pity on a bruised and battered little girl.

As my father's voice grew louder, my sobbing intensified. He picked me up off the ground by one arm and began dragging me back to the car. As I struggled to regain my legs under me to take the pressure off my arm, I could hear the once-soft voice of the woman turn to yelling and shrieking in a mixture of confusion and shock. I said nothing as we drove home, my father screaming the entire time about how inept I was at everything.

When I think back on this incident, I wonder what this stranger must have been thinking. She saw a six-year-old girl roll out of a vehicle traveling 25-30 mph and into her pseudo-mansion yard. Then, while she was talking to the girl, a man came up, grabbed the little girl by the arm, dragged her back into a vehicle and sped off. Did she ever call the police? Has she ever wondered what happened to me?

CHAPTER THREE
COME ON, MARLENE

*"She's mad but she's magic. There's no lie
in her fire."* —Charles Bukowski

MY MOTHER WAS A FREE SPIRIT, a lost and wandering gypsy,
who moved from one job to another. She moved one place to another,
one relationship to another. I absolutely idolized her. She was tall,
5'11", with curves that could make heads turn. I was born when she
was barely 21. When she wasn't using drugs or strung out, she was
breathtaking. She had soft hands, and the type of milky white skin
that burned more than it tanned. Her dirty blonde hair had a gentle,
natural wave that most women spent hours with a hairdresser or
curling iron to achieve. My mother had eyes that appeared blue on
some days, hazel on others. She smelled of Jovan Musk for Woman
perfume, and cigarettes. No matter how little money we had, she
always had money for a fresh pack of Kool cigarettes. Many times
she sent me to the nearest corner store, with a handwritten note, to
purchase them for her.

My mother spoke like a woman who had spent too much time
in military towns and truck stops. I learned early that language and
its subtleties could be used, both as a weapon and as a way for my
mother to control those around her. Often she used words to belittle
me. I lived in a constant state of fear of her criticism, chastised if I
read too much, chided if I read too little. I was berated for not cutting
my sandwich the proper way, or for holding my knife incorrectly. I
was lambasted for the way I held a trash bag. I was reprimanded for
not drying the dishes with accuracy and precision. I was told my feel-

ings were insignificant and that because I was a child, I didn't know or understand anything. It usually came out something like this: "You are so fucking stupid. When are you going to grow up and get your shit together and understand that we love each other, and everything can't be about you?" In my mind that meant: "*I'm an idiot who can't be trusted, and nobody cares about me.*"

My mother never confided in me, never shared her reasons for anything. If I asked what was going on, or shared my concerns about a boyfriend, it was discounted. I was often told "You have no right to feel that way," or "These things are for adults to understand, and you don't know how you really feel."

Her moods changed often and without warning. One moment she was caring and interested in what I was reading, and then without notice she would slap me, or yell at me and tell me how useless I was. She always paid more attention to the needs and wants of whatever man was around. That was my dad, or if they were on the outs, her boyfriend of the day. But her tone was always short with me, and it was clear that most of the time I was an afterthought. I was the third wheel that made her less attractive to men, not to mention less mobile.

Awoken one night by the laughs and chuckles coming from the living room, I came out of my room to get water and to see what was happening. I had been under strict instructions to stay in my room, but like most nights, I couldn't help myself. As I rounded the corner, I saw a strange man, belly hanging out and covered in tattoos, sitting on the couch. My mother had her back towards me. She sat straddled over his lap, topless. He paused for a moment, awkwardly. "Oh hey, I didn't know you had a kid here," he stammered, reaching for the gun and the pile of white dust and pills sprawled over the coffee table in an attempt to hide them.

"Her?" my mother asked. "I wouldn't worry about her. She's a fucking idiot and useless." She turned toward me, her eyes glaring, and said, "I told you not to leave your fucking room. Get back in there and stay there." I slithered back into my room.

Despite incidents like these, I would always be so glad when my dad was gone. When they were on the outs, the strain was lifted, the mood lighter. My mother would briefly take an interest in me. But it would only last moments, until my parents ended up back together again or until she met another man. In my eyes, some of my mom's new boyfriends seemed better than my dad, even if they later turned out to be drug dealers, con men, petty thieves or even worse, abusers.

Once, my mother roused me from a sound sleep in the middle of the night. Another move, I thought, but something seemed different this time. My mother was more stressed than usual, she seemed scared, even paranoid. She cried as we drove aimlessly to a truck stop. She loved truck stops; the food, the convenience, the drugs and the men. It didn't take her long to attract a lonely man on the road away from his family. She climbed up into his truck for a little while, leaving me alone in the car with the bright lights of the parking lot shining on me. I closed my eyes, head buried in Love Bunny's chest, and waited. It seemed scary, mysterious and also cool.

She returned with quick cash for gas, drugs and our escape in return for her trip up to his cab.

My mom seemed the master of our destiny, using her cunning skills to get men to give her what we needed. She was a magnet for attention. It was amazing to me how she could drop everything and go someplace new without any thought or care. A fresh start, a new life was always only a car ride away. A new city, a new garbage bag suitcase.

My mom never had a steady job. Often, I had no idea she was even working. But, one of her many jobs was in the dry cleaning department at the Dunes Hotel in Las Vegas. In the late 1970s and early 1980s, Vegas was still the "it" party place to be seen. She often encountered celebrities and loved to brag about her interactions with them.

In November of 1979, "Marvelous" Marvin Hagler was in town for his first shot at the World Middleweight Champion belt. This was a big deal, because Marvin Hagler and his family had moved to Brockton, Massachusetts, my dad's hometown, after the Newark riots in 1967. He had been my father's favorite fighter, and my father had watched him fight in the small gyms around Brockton and in Cape Cod where he grew up. My mother met Marvin Hagler and even received a signed photo that my father cherished. In the end, the championship fight was declared a draw, and the champ retained his belt. Although my father was upset, his cherished photo seemed to help.

One morning shortly after the fights, while I was watching Picture Pages, the show was interrupted with news on a fire at the Dunes. For a brief moment I wasn't sure if my mom had gone to work that morning. As I stood up I heard the shower, and realized it was her day off. She wasn't in the fire, and I remember feeling both relieved and sad. Already I was wishing myself out of being raised by my parents. When they were home, I spent most of my time locked in my room, hiding, talking to imaginary and stuffed friends. I daydreamed about becoming an orphan, and being taken away to live with a real family. I wanted my own Daddy Warbucks from *Little Orphan Annie*, who dreamed of having a wonderful daughter to call his own. Each day, I was met with the cold hard reality that these were my parents, and this was my life.

Although I have no proof, I always thought that my mom started the fire or was involved somehow. She seemed too calm when I told her what was happening on the television. Within a week, we had moved again.

My mother never had a solid career path. She worked at a paint factory in one city, then dry cleaners, and sometimes she had no job at all. The most ambitious she got was to train as a dental hygienist. I remember her studying for tests. I tried to help by giving studying hints as best as I could. But like everything else in her life, that didn't last either.

In my house, it was expected that you never talked about reality to other people. Inventing stories to cover for the truth was the expectation, and fear of not doing a good enough job kept you constantly motivated. This was the way of life on which my parents insisted, and the sooner that was accepted, the easier it would be. Often, I wished that woman could have rescued me from my parents, but she didn't. Nobody ever did.

CHAPTER FOUR
HIDING IN THE OPEN

"Just because I let you go, doesn't mean
I wanted to." —Unknown

ON ANY GIVEN DAY, I could walk into the house and my mother could greet me with, "Get the atlas. Where do you want to go next?"

We had a giant Rand McNally Atlas that seemed as big and tall as I was. Each state had its own page, and the interstates and highways fanned out like a giant spider's web. I spent hours playing with this book in my room alone. Each of its pages held my dreams of escape, the hopes of a new start and a new chance in our next location. I fantasized that the next correctly picked location could become our chance at happiness.

I looked over each page, carefully studying the roads and running my fingertips over the expressways, as if they were cars driving to their next destination. I would carefully consider my options, often taking hours to flip through the pages. I wanted to be near water, either lakes or oceans was fine with me. With each move, I held hope that the new location would have what we were looking for, whatever it was. With each move came the promise from my mom that things would be better, and I held hope each time that she might be right.

In the end, it didn't matter where I chose. The decision was never really mine. Depending on the day, I might have five minutes or five hours to say my goodbyes to any friends or acquaintances I might have. Usually there wasn't time, and truthfully I never knew what to say anyway. I was more concerned about packing my things, my stuffed friends. I had grown tired of leaving things behind, so I began to take more care. My mother and I would hop onto the nearest expressway in our clunker and drive until she couldn't drive anymore. We always stopped at a Love's Truck Stop, where she would order a Patty Melt and Diet Coke before hitting the road again. Wherever we stopped was our new home. San Diego, Los Angeles, Las Vegas, Salt Lake City, Denver, Boulder were a few of the cities where we stayed, but not for long.

I often wondered, *"What are we running from? Is my mother a criminal? Did she get fired? Did we owe the landlord money? What about school? Was this my family?"* Years of daytime television had made me wonder whether I had been kidnapped from my real family. Nothing about me seemed to fit in, and as I grew older the constant meandering was wearing thin.

Sometimes I felt like the great adventurers I had read about in books, Lewis and Clark or Tom Sawyer. But our perpetual moving came with a price. In kindergarten, we moved twice early in the school year, landing back in San Diego. My class was scheduled to go to Sea World the next day. I was in love with Jacques Cousteau and never missed his television specials. His adventures aboard the ship *Calypso* made me want to spend my life on the ocean. A trip to Sea World seemed serendipitous: I had just started at the school the day before, and could immediately go on a field trip to my favorite place on Earth. But my mom was already itching to hit the road again. Another move, another garbage bag suitcase. No Sea World, no surprise. I was frustrated.

After my years with Bill Cosby and Picture Pages, I was initially excited when I finally got to go to school. But I never attended the same school for more than two or three months at a time, and often was lucky to make it two weeks. My mom would register me for a school on Friday, and by Monday we would move. I spent one day in some schools, if I showed at all.

But I loved school when I got to go, and it became my escape. Even though nobody knew me, even though it was a strange place with strange teachers, I loved it. I would rise by myself, get dressed and walk to school. No one ever made sure that I arrived to school on time, or even attended for that matter. But, it was better than being at home. I ate two real meals there, breakfast and lunch. Nobody intimidated me over how much I was eating and what I was eating. It was a blessed relief and escape.

I had learned to blend in at school. Like my dad, I never asked too many questions, never achieved too high of grades, always played it safe in the middle. I lived for Mondays, and always tried to find a way to stay at school longer, even resorting to taking the long way home after classes. Weekends and school breaks were torture. I had to spend all that time at home, without knowing whether or not I would be fed, or yelled at, or hit, or see my mom beaten. I was usually locked in my room, either with a real lock from the outside or with a verbal one from my parents. I read and dreamed about how my next escape would be better.

My half-brother, Allen, lived with us off and on for years. I have scattered memories of him sometimes being there, and sometimes not. He was a very angry boy, but most times my ally. We had a common adversary, our parents.

My mother had Allen when she was barely 17. She split up with his dad, Big Al, a year later. Big Al had custody of Allen, no doubt so my mother could continue to live her free spirit lifestyle. Big Al remarried and had two more children before his untimely death from a forklift accident at work. His second wife couldn't keep Allen because my mother refused, so he ended up coming and going and eventually staying with us. Allen brought a paycheck with him, social security money from his father's passing. And at the age of 18, he was to receive a sizable settlement as a result of Big Al's death. This money, and the subsequent settlement trust fund, became the core of many of the arguments surrounding my brother and parents. I was useless, a drain on everyone and everything. Allen, at least, paid the rent.

My brother was five years older than me. Even though he teased and tortured me like a big brother, I needed him. But Allen had the type of temper that comes from being bullied at school, beaten at home, and an inability to properly grieve the loss of a parent.

I was in the second grade, and we were living with my mother somewhere in Colorado. We had been there for a month at most, having moved from Las Vegas, one of several moves in and out of Vegas over the years. Allen had just reappeared again. While walking home from school, an older Hispanic boy named Paco tried to show me a hand-drawn picture of a penis. Allen came to my rescue. His temper kicked in, and he screamed, "What the hell are you doing? She's a little girl!"

Paco and his friends laughed and said something in Spanish. Then they said, "Fuck off, puto" (pussy) to Allen, and Paco pulled out a small switchblade. As the knife flipped open, the other boys chanted and jeered at Allen and me. A fight was on. I wasn't scared. Confrontations like this were common in our neighborhoods and schools, and my brother was usually involved.

Allen took off his jacket and wrapped it around his left arm. It was starting to look like a scene from West Side Story. Paco lunged towards Allen with the knife, but Allen's coat deflected the blade. With Paco off balance, Allen struck Paco in the face with his fist, knocking him to the ground. Allen, big for his age and twice the size of Paco, pounced on him and wildly swung at him, hitting him over and over, until finally the other boys pulled Allen off and threw him to the ground. Then Allen picked up part of a cinder block and threw it at the boys. This bought us enough time to run home and lock the door. We didn't leave the house for weeks, afraid of retaliation, and we never told our parents.

We knew that another move would be coming soon. And, two months later, we moved again.

Allen and I were hungry, a lot. Food was often forgotten in the house. There were usually empty cupboards and a bare refrigerator. On a good day, I could make a mayonnaise sandwich, with no cold cuts, but it was unlikely. Eating also required asking for permission. Asking my father for anything, even food, set me up for a litany of insults, mockery and taunts. The belittling and antagonizing made it easier to go hungry.

Eventually my brother and I resorted to stealing newspapers out of newspaper boxes. We would put in a dime, open the door and take all the papers, which we would then sell door-to-door. We would use the money to buy food, mostly candy at the corner store.

In one neighborhood, the store was next to the school playground. If we were careful and a bit daring we could climb onto the roof of the store from the jungle gym and break into the building to steal food. We did what we had to do.

My dad's ridicule and mockery led to a lot of psychological games with us, the ones involving food seemed the most torturous. One day he bought ice cream and asked us if we would like some. I turned it down, knowing that my father never bought treats, and if he did they were not for us. But Allen, new to my dad's ways, and always hungry, accepted. "Yeah, I'll have some." I thought he was a fool to fall for this trick.

Happily my dad gave him a bowl and watched, smirking, a gleam in his eye. Allen ate a spoonful, and then another. My dad, in practical hysterics as this point, couldn't take it anymore. He slapped Allen on the back of the head.

"Why did you hit me?" Allen asked.

"Because it's ice cream for dogs, you fucking idiot!" Dad had set us up for a big prank. I had known better than to fall for it, but Allen was still learning.

All I could think was: *"He bought ice cream for the dog, and not us?"* It wasn't completely shocking, but I added it as just another in a long list of reasons I was mentally compiling on why I was always happy when mom would say we were moving and Dad wasn't coming. It was a relief.

Unfortunately, he always reappeared.

My dad was probably scared of Allen. He was growing up to be bigger than my dad, and he had a terrible temper, getting into fist fights at school on an almost weekly basis. So my dad sought to keep him under his thumb. My brother, regardless of how big he was physically, was terrified of him. I was too. He was unpredictable. Nice in one moment, and then without warning, he would snap.

Our parents struggled to put food on the table, and alcohol, drugs and partying with friends were a bigger priority for them than keeping us fed. What small amount of food that Allen and I were given needed to be rationed. We always wanted more. Especially Allen. We were so hungry that Allen would often pack a bag in the morning, claiming that he didn't like the school lunch. The truth was that he would eat this lunch on the way to school as breakfast; and then eat the school lunch later. One day, as we walked the six blocks to school, Allen was munching on his lunch. Just as he was about to throw the evidence into a garbage can, my father drove up. He was caught. The punishment was severe. No food, at all, for three days.

I was punished as well, no food for a week. It had been decided that my punishment would be more severe because I was covering up and lying for my brother, and that type of behavior couldn't be tolerated. It was confusing; I had thought we were supposed to cover for each other. It appeared that my father didn't want my brother and me getting too close, and he could change the rules any time.

When my parents weren't home, Allen would sneak around the kitchen looking for something — anything — to eat. He climbed onto the counters, and dug in the small cabinet above the refrigerator, the one nobody could reach. Once in, he found several boxes of Cracker Jacks hidden, and clearly off limits to us. But my brother was hungry, and so he swiped two boxes. He hurried them off to our room, and against my wishes and protests that this was a bad idea, he sat on his bed, tore open the boxes and began to devour their contents. I warned him again that we were going to get into big trouble, pointing out how difficult it was going to be to hide the evidence. Finally, after binging on the boxes and realizing his mistake, he began to panic. Quickly he took the toys from the opened and emptied boxes, then hid them under his bed. There was no way he could put them back already opened, and the trash was clearly an obvious place to hide the packages.

It turned out this had been another trap, designed by my dad to test the will of two hungry children. We failed, and we paid. Our parents came home and marched to the cabinet. Were we under surveillance? How could they know so quickly? I could hear my father stomping around the kitchen, and I knew all hell was about to break loose.

I listened with fear as his feet marched down the hallway, growing louder and louder as he approached. Stomp, stomp, stomp. My heart was racing, tears welling just as they had when I had "fallen" from the truck. We had just finished our punishment for the lunch incident, so I could only imagine how severe this one would be.

The door swung open. "Who ate my Cracker Jacks?!" I sat up in bed, eyes wide, but said nothing. I could see the perspiration starting on my father's forehead. My brother stared blankly. I knew what was coming. My father ranted and raved for nearly twenty minutes. When it was clear that neither my brother nor I were going to confess, he stormed off in a huff. Had our silence paid off?

I breathed a sigh of relief, thinking we might get away unpunished. "See, I told you," I whispered. "You should have just left them alone." I barely finished my sentence when my father appeared out of nowhere. He had been listening outside the door, and was ready to dole out the punishment. Since neither of us would confess, both of us were held responsible. As with the lunch incident, the issues didn't matter, so we were both punished. If Allen fought in school, we were both grounded. If Allen talked back, we were both regulated to our bedroom. If Allen didn't properly wash a dish, then we had to rewash every dish in the house since I had dried the dish and put it away without noticing.

It turns out my brother had left footprints on the countertop, the evidence was too convincing for us to deny. The punishment was unrelenting. We would spend one week locked in our room. The only time we were allowed out was to use the bathroom, and we had to ask permission to have access. You can imagine how often we wanted to do that. The punishment included no food. In my father's mind, we had eaten enough Cracker Jacks to last us that long.

The final part of the punishment was inflicted on me, and me alone. In the middle of the night, I woke up with terrible stomach cramps. As I lay in agony, I couldn't decide if I should get up and get my mother, knowing that waking her would incur additional punishment. I ended up having diarrhea all over my nightclothes and bed. I immediately knew I was in trouble. Before I even got out of bed, I was trying to think of ways to cover my tracks. I quietly got off the top bunk and started crawling around the room, looking for clothes. I must not have been as quiet as I thought, because my mom came rushing into the room. I had forgotten that they had friends over. When the door burst open I was standing there half-naked, with feces all over me. She began laughing and pointing, and told me that I needed to get back in bed and lay in it until morning. Ashamed, I began crawling up the steps of the bunk beds. This left my brother to gag over the smell, and me cold and petrified, alone with Love Bunny. It was a sleepless night. It was also after this incident that I first remember having problems with insomnia, a problem that I still experience today, especially if I am feeling stressed or anxiety.

In the beginning, my brother and I thought the lock-down would be a breeze compared to other punishments that we had endured. At least we were together, and we didn't have to be around our parents, a fate we both loathed. The first day was simple enough. We talked and played board games quietly to pass the time. It was a typical day. The next day was more difficult, as our bodies began to react to the lack of food. We began drinking out of the sink when we used the bathroom to try and minimize the empty feelings in our stomachs. By the third day, we were in agony, Allen more than me. His size wasn't helping him. We were practically permanent fixtures in the bathroom, our heads in the toilet, vomiting until there was nothing left but stomach bile. This continued for four more days until we had served out our sentence.

No one asked why we missed school. We never told anyone.

We moved again.

The mind games seemed to increase with the amount of drugs my parents were using. Maybe they thought it was a parenting style. They would often leave us home alone, always with the same instructions: "We're going out and won't be home until you're in bed. Don't leave the house, and be in bed by 10." I always rolled my eyes. It was becoming increasingly more difficult to listen to my parents. Half the time they couldn't remember what they said, and would make up or change the rules without warning. If they wanted to punish you they would find a reason, or make up a reason. I didn't dare show signs of annoyance. They would leave, and my brother and I would do what we normally did, which was whatever we wanted. We were seven and twelve at the time.

After my parents left, my brother and I would peer from behind the curtains and watch as they drove away. We waited another ten minutes, just for good measure. Then, we left. Out the front door, we took to the streets in search of neighborhood kids. Sometimes we played football, baseball, soccer, or tag, whatever the other kids were in the mood to do. We were just looking for a way to escape.

Once we had been outside fifteen minutes when someone shouted "car!" As we picked up our cardboard bases and began moving to the side of the street, my brother and I looked at each other, faces frozen in panic. Our parents. We attempted to race home, but our violation wouldn't go unnoticed. We saw our parents pulling up, and knew the punishment would be brutal. Another test, failed.

I am not sure I could describe my relationship with my brother as a friendship. We were five years apart in age, and since he wasn't always around, we seemed more like cell mates who watched out for each other. But the guards were always making sure we didn't get too close, and we were unable to hatch any real scheme to escape. With our constant moving, I had all but given up on making friends, real friends.

But I did have one true friend: Love Bunny. Love Bunny was a gangly white stuffed rabbit. Like the White Rabbit in *Alice in Won-*

37

derland, Love Bunny seemed to be the most logical out of all the characters in my life. The rabbit had been with me since I was a baby, and was the only thing I had that brought me feelings of safety, comfort and companionship. Lots of children have a stuffed animal or blanket that they can't sleep without. Love Bunny was not only that comfort, but also the only one who ever knew the truth.

Love Bunny had come to life for me. We often had conversations about kids at school, hunger, boredom, and on occasion we discussed escape plans. We often spoke about the future, and more than once I made promises of how our life would be. The future was where I found hope.

I had hope that things could be different and would be different. I would hope that with the next move, my mother would be different, that life would be different. Every move brought with it the chance of a new and fresh start. Hope that we would stay. Hope that my mother would find and work a steady job. Hope that the fights, parties and neglect would end. Hope that my dad, who I had come to loathe, would disappear. I often talked of college with Love Bunny. I would argue that college wasn't possible for me/us. Yet she would direct and guide me to that very possibility. She always offered great and motherly advice in return. When I think back to my conversations with this rabbit, it is with fondness, the fondness of reminiscing one has with friends and family, recalling the glory days. Love Bunny was the only one who knew the truth, the whole truth, and loved me anyway.

It was also that white bunny, yellowed over the years by wear and by my tears, which gave me the strength to continue on in life. On more than one occasion I remember crying into Love Bunny's belly, saddened that my mother never returned home from a party to celebrate my birthday as promised. I was afraid of starving to death, afraid that one of my mother's boyfriends would kill her during an argument, afraid that if I made the slightest noise the same wrath would fall upon me. There was nonstop anxiety and dread that both my mother and the man of the day would lose composure, and that as a result I would never be heard from again. I had an immutable fear, walking home from school each day, that everyone and everything would be gone when I returned home. I was never sure if it would be better or worse if they disappeared without me. Me, forgotten, alone forever. In those moments, it was Love Bunny who comforted and consoled me. She was the only one I could truly confide in, the only one who I knew understood me more than anyone else.

Love Bunny would shake her head when my parents would punish me, starve me, fall down drunk, or get high in front of me, and say, "Adults are not supposed to act like this." She was the reminder. The constant. The voice in my head, in my gut, that gave me strength when I had none. She was the reason to keep fighting. That stuffed animal became my only true advocate.

She would console me and tell me, "Things are going to get better." I would wipe the tears away, make a promise that they would be, and then crack open a book and disappear into the story.

CHAPTER FIVE
ENDLESS AMOUNTS OF FIRST DAYS

"You will never get a second chance
to make a first impression" —Unknown

THEY SAY THERE'S NOTHING like a first impression, and with my name, I always give a strange one.

I grew up in an era when girls were named Jennifer, Amy, Heather, Melissa and Michelle. People didn't name kids after places the way they do now, like Madison, Brooklyn, Montana, Cheyenne, or use last names as first names. Everything was practical and traditional in spelling and pronunciation. It seemed everything about my name brought me grief. Every town I moved to and every new school I started, I got strange looks when I introduced myself. "What kind of a name is *that*?"

I set out to change the not-so-nice reactions. After all, each new school offered me a chance at a fresh start. So I began to suggest nicknames. My father had often referred to me as Sam, I was never sure why unless he was projecting his desire for a boy and his own dissatisfaction of my name. My teacher at the time promptly rejected the suggestion. There were too many Jessicas, Jennifers and Sarahs in class already; I couldn't win. I tried another tactic at the next school, and told the teacher that I'd rather go by my middle name. People do that all the time. The teacher seemed on board. The only problem was it wasn't just my first name that was uncommon. My middle name was non-existent. I was forced again to stick with Shenandoah.

There was nowhere to hide. I was a small girl with a big, unwieldy, uncommon name. I was also a girl who never stayed in one place long enough to let people know I was more than just a silly name. The jeers were unrelenting.

We had moved for the umpteenth time. We had been in numerous towns within Michigan by this time, my mother's home state. I assumed she wanted or needed to be closer to her extended family, but she also had a terrible fight with my father. We had taken a cross-country Greyhound bus ride that felt like it lasted months. I ate crackers and spray-can cheese the entire trip. The bus smelled like a port-a-potty, and there were strange people who talked to themselves. I was seriously scared by the experience, and vowed never to travel by bus again.

My mother and I landed at her sister's house. It didn't take long for my father to reappear weeks later.

We lived first in Grand Haven, then several other locations in and around the Muskegon area located on the Lake Michigan coastline. Like many of Michigan's small cities during the 1980s, Muskegon was economically devastated by the ongoing industrial and automotive downturn. By all definitions it was an urban setting, rife with the typical problems of cities whose citizens are out of work. It was perhaps most famous for being the birthplace of the evangelical Christian television host Jim Bakker.

My father started his own landscaping business there, which provided some stability for us, and after six or seven more moves, we eventually landed in a small house on Dale Street. It wasn't fancy, but it was our own. This was the first time my parents had purchased their own home and, for a moment, it felt like things were changing. My parents had initially sent me to a Catholic school. Not because they were religious; clearly their lifestyle did not conform to any religion. I can only assume it was their way of trying to give me a better education. The house was located in a rough neighborhood, and the public schools were known for their problems. This was the first time it felt like my parents were trying, actually trying, to get their act together.

It seemed as though the partying had slowed down. After a friend's bachelor party, my dad swore he would never drink again. He was getting too old to recover, he claimed. And he did seem to ease up.

The experiment was short lived. On my first day at school, I was asked to write a paper on my parents' heroes. The idea seemed completely ridiculous to me. Did my parents even have heroes? We never talked about anything of substance, and I had no idea how was I ever going to complete the assignment. In my house, you couldn't just ask the question, listen to the response and write the paper. It was never that simple. So I did what I did best, I lied. I wrote a paper on my dad's made-up hero, Babe Ruth, and my mother's imaginary hero, Marilyn Monroe. But in my conservative Catholic school, writing about Marilyn's sexual magnetism didn't go over so well. That, coupled with my parents' unwillingness to come to mass and my constant inability to wear the proper uniform, meant I was soon transferred to the local public school. However, local politics forced school lines to be redrawn, and after six months I was transferred to yet another elementary school across town. After that, I tested out of my grade level for reading and ended up in the library doing my work. Alone.

When my mother was around, we had a forced "let's spend time together" routine. I jumped at the chance, because I loathed being around my father. His rages and anger grew increasingly difficult to deal with, so I took any chance to escape from having to be near him. Being together with my mother often meant that I would sit on the toilet seat and read aloud from whatever book I was reading at the time, while she bathed in the tub.

When I finally reached the sixth grade things began to change in many ways. We were still living at the Dale house, and I would ride my bike to the public library by myself and stay for hours. No one ever asked where I was, and the librarians always had new book selections for me. I read things that were popular at the time, all the Beverly Clearly books (*Ralph and the Motorcycle* was a favorite), Judy Blume's books, *Sarah, Plain and Tall*, the *Indian in the Cupboard*, *Jacob Have I Loved*, Shel Silverstein's books, and much more. As I started getting a little older, maybe around sixth grade or so, I started reading Stephen King books, and then, because my mom had read them, I started reading books by John Jakes. That led me to reading many autobiographical and history books.

Then, after starting at the public school, I met Saralyn. We became quick friends, something that simply didn't happen to me. Saralyn and I had a lot in common. Her parents were divorced, and she and her mother lived in a small apartment together. She saw her dad every other weekend. We both dreaded those weekends.

Her mom worked and was rarely at home, which left Saralyn alone and unsupervised. We would spend all of our time together, and relish the weekends when we could have sleepovers at her house. Sleepovers were not allowed at my house, which was fine. I would not have wanted to bring friends over to see the sad state of our lives or subject them to the cruelty of my parents.

Saralyn and I didn't talk much about our parents or our home lives. She never asked about mine and I never asked about hers. We both just knew. It was easy for us to fend for ourselves, and we spent our time gossiping, talking and plotting, mostly about the future.

In sixth grade passing notes in class was all the rage. It was popular to write ,"Do you like me? Check 'yes' or 'no.'" Through our constant note writing, Sara and I invented ever-more intricate ways to fold a piece of paper. We would write each other's name on the front, and enlist our classmates to pass the notes. It was the first and the last time that I felt like I truly belonged with a group of my peers. Sara complained daily on the playground that I needed a shorter name, because it wouldn't fit on our origami-style notes. So she began testing nicknames. At first it was "Sh--------," but we both quickly realized that wasn't going to work. It almost looked like it could be mistaken for a curse word. Then one day she wrote "Shen," and it stuck. From that moment on, people started calling me Shen. At the time, I didn't have a clue what Shen meant, nor did I care. It was close enough to Jen that people never seemed to question it in the same way. I just wanted a change, and Shen was fine with me.

Like most kids, I was always looking for my name on the customizable key chains and other trinkets found in truck stops across the nation. It didn't take long for me to realize that the chances of finding my name were nil. In second grade, I had a friend who did a Show and Tell about her name. She had a framed poster that was in a fancy script explaining the origin of her name, all the famous people who shared her name, etc. I was interested, and wanted to know more about my name. I was stuck with an old copy of the Encyclopedia Britannica from the school library. The closest I could find was "Shenandoah National Park." That was not what I was looking for.

It would be nearly 20 years before I ran into a Native American man, a client, who was able to shed some light on my name. He explained because so many different tribes lived in the Shenandoah Valley the name had several meanings. River Through the Spruces. River of High Mountains. Silver Waters. Given we were applying it to me, he suggested we might settle on his favorite: "Beautiful Daughter of the Stars." And so there it was, finally an appropriate definition I could share with others.

So Shenandoah translated to Beautiful Daughter of the Stars. Truthfully, although I knew it meant something beautiful, it was still hard to relate it to me. I never saw myself as anything close to the beauty in a star, though I did like the greater universal meaning and context. By this time, everyone was calling me Shen. To this day so many people know me as Shen that when I'm referred to as Shenandoah I can get confused looks.

I once met a business contact at a restaurant, who at the end of our lunch said, "Shen. That's an interesting name. Do you know what it means?"

I was curious, but fearful at the same time. It was clear from our conversation that she had a grasp of Chinese medical language, being an expert in the area. "Um...no. It doesn't mean something bad, does it?" I asked, sheepishly. My first thought was that it was some terrible disease. How appalling would that be, walking around calling yourself tuberculosis or some other equivalent?

"You don't? Well, when you get back to the office you should look it up." She smiled.

"Or you could just tell me, because now I'm really nervous." I'm not known for my patience, and the anticipation of finding out was now overwhelming.

"Check it out when you get back." Damn, she wasn't going to give it away. "Let me know what you think."

I tried a few more times to pry the information from her as I waited for the check, with no luck. The restaurant was only a few minutes from the office, but the entire drive back I wracked my mind, thinking of all the terrible and horrible things it could mean. When I got to the office, I ran into the building and back to my computer. I couldn't open Google fast enough.

Define Shen, I typed. I watched as Google did its algorithms, an eternity it seemed, but within milliseconds there stood the answer: *Shen (in Chinese thought) is the spiritual element of a person's psyche.* Not bad, I thought to myself. *Spirit, god, deity, spiritual, supernatural, awareness, consciousness, etc.* As I read, a sense of disbelief began to overwhelm me. Relief at first that I wasn't associated with some debilitating disease, but that quickly dissipated. I stopped reading and sat for a long moment.

I had spent years hating my name. I'd tried everything to change it. Then suddenly, in the midst of transforming my life and changing careers, I found this. My name finally became a part of me, for the first time in my life. I felt that I was where I was supposed to be, at the exact time I was supposed to be there.

I wish I had known the meaning of my name sooner. I spent so much time looking for what was special about me, and perhaps the answer was with me the whole time, in the one thing I hated most. It's odd. I remember hearing people tell me I was special; I was just never treated that way. My mother told me I was special, so it's easy to see why I wouldn't, or couldn't, believe it. I had convinced myself that I wasn't special. In fact, I spent my whole life doing everything

I could to be average. When people asked me what I was good at, I would always shrug and say, "Nothing."

Much changed in that sixth grade classroom. My teacher, Mr. Derby, the only elementary school teacher whose name I actually remember, told me that I was special. Most of the kids were disappointed to find out they had Mr. Derby; he was known as the tough teacher, the one who didn't take any nonsense. Most of the kids seemed nervous to have him. But he appreciated the work I did in class and praised me. He said he had a feeling I would be an important person in the world. At the time, I wondered, *"Doesn't he know my background? Doesn't he know I don't have any skills or abilities? Doesn't he know I'm destined to be a good-for-nothing drug addicted wandering gypsy, like my mother?"*

I had friends and acquaintances with obvious talents in one thing or another, such as playing an instrument, acting, writing, singing, sports. Everyone around me seemed to excel at something, but not me. My brother was a fantastic artist and good at soccer. When my mom wasn't high on drugs or drunk, she was very personable and a great storyteller. Those talents had carried her far in life. She was also a looker and men adored her. But me? I had nothing. I had spent years riding the middle, hiding in plain sight.

It's amazing what one compliment can do in a person's life. This one compliment forever changed the way I looked at myself. His words stuck with me, "You're special." I would repeat them over and over in my mind, and replay the conversation for Love Bunny. In my bedroom at night, I would daydream about my life. I would confide in my friends about my desire to go to college. They all questioned college, kids from our neighborhood should feel lucky to just get a job, after all. But my determination grew to escape the low expectations that the world had set for me, that I had set for myself. These words, these precious words, were the first positive recognition I had ever received.

Believing I was special made it even more difficult when I had to lie to Mr. Derby. "Shen, can I see you in the hallway?" His voice was gruff and firm, and I knew what was coming next. It happened every semester, at every school. Each new teacher handled it differently, yet it always felt the same to me. As I got up from my desk, I began to slowly walk towards the door. Behind me, I could hear the other kids snickering and laughing. There was only one reason to be summoned into the hall. You had done something so severe that the teacher didn't want to or couldn't mention it in front of the other children.

I could see the disappointment in my teacher's eyes. I knew what he was about to ask. And he said, "Shen, where is your report card? I've asked you to have it signed and brought back to school for the last several weeks. You said your parents were coming to conferences, and they didn't show, and when I sent your report card home, you said you would return it within a few days. What is the problem?"

He was right. I did tell him that my parents would be coming to conferences, and I knew it was a lie. My parents had never attended a parent teacher conference. I knew this one would be no different. But I was afraid to say anything other than, "Of course, they are looking forward to it." It was easier than the truth. Later, when they didn't show, I had made an excuse about them having to work late or something about car trouble. These types of excuses always seemed to suffice with other teachers. But Mr. Derby was different. He seemed to genuinely care that my parents had missed the conference, and was adamant when he requested that I take my report card home and return it, signed by my parents.

"How exactly am I going to accomplish that?" I wondered. Most kids are scared to bring their report card home if they are failing, or if the teacher leaves a comment about not listening in class or skipping school. But that was not the problem I was having. In fact, the report card in question had straight A's, and my teacher made glowing remarks about my attendance and work ethic. The problem was getting 20 minutes of my parents' time to show them the report card, and then to have them actually sign it. I had already made several unsuccessful attempts.

On my first attempt, I stayed up until nearly 11:00 p.m. waiting for my mother to come home. When she finally returned, she was in a drunken stupor. She slurred that whatever it was would have to wait until morning. I woke up early the next morning, hoping to catch her, but she was still sound asleep as I left for school. A few days later I tried again, but in the middle of the discussion my father came home and a fight ensued. I was disappointed. None of my efforts worked.

So here I was, stuck in the hallway with my teacher pressing me on why I hadn't produced my signed report card. I did what I did best. I lied. I had gotten really good at it over the years. It always made me feel terrible, but I rationalized that it was never over important details. I tried to keep the lies to matters involving my family, why we were moving, or where my parents were, but it was becoming more difficult the longer we stayed in one place.

"I keep forgetting to give it to them," I began. When I first began lying my voice had been shaky, but with all the practice over the years I had become more convincing. "I promise that I will write myself a note and stick it in my backpack and be sure to ask my parents tonight at dinner and I will bring it back first thing tomorrow."

"OK," my teacher said. I could tell by his voice that he was frustrated with me, but as most of my teachers had done before, he gave me the benefit of the doubt because I was generally well-behaved. But he continued, "If you don't have it tomorrow, you will be asked to go back home and get it, or I'm going to stop by your home after school and talk to your parents myself."

This was serious. Neither of those options were going to end well, for either of us. That night, as I lay in bed, I contemplated all of my choices. I could ask my parents, but given the tension in the house lately I knew that would only end in more discipline for me. The punishments had begun to escalate. On a previous evening, leading up to asking for a signature on my report card, I had made the mistake of lying on the living room floor. I heard the dogs scratching at the door, and when I rose to let them in I must have stood in front of my father, who was watching television. He became irate. He lunged towards me, fork in hand, missing my head but stabbing the fork into my upper left shoulder. "You're in the way!" he screamed. I cowered down, holding my shoulder, and silently went into my room. I used an old t-shirt to stop the bleeding. No one ever spoke of the incident.

On the nights when my parents were home and sober, interrupting their television time would end with a verbal lashing. There was nothing I needed that would ever rise above the needs of my parents. Given their past behaviors, I had become intimidated to even ask for the smallest of items.

My other option was to do nothing, and allow my teacher to come to my house and meet my parents. That clearly would land me in trouble, because one of my parents would be drunk, high and belligerent, and the police would be called. In my family, the cops were seen as the devil. They were people to be distrusted, and not turned to, in times of crisis. They were always referred to as "pigs."

The third and only other choice I could come up with was to forge my mother's signature.

It seems a bit extreme, I know. I was 11 at the time, and it wasn't the first time I had signed my mother's name. I had done it multiple times, to participate in a spelling bee, to go on field trips, and even to be in a school play. I actually practiced the skill in my spare time, because I never knew when it would be called upon. As I was lying in my room, I began to practice again. After 100 or so attempts, I decided it was time to try it out on the real document.

The real test of a forgery always comes when you have to submit it. I was panicked as I handed it over to Mr. Derby, because unlike other people, I really wanted him to like me. I thought it best to get to school early, and slip it onto his desk before he arrived. When he came in that morning he glanced in my direction, and I merely pointed. He walked over, picked up my report card and examined it for a signature, and then put it back on his desk, distracted by students as they walked in.

It worked. It actually worked! The commotion of the morning routine worked. I was clear again. I had managed to survive another close call. But it was getting more difficult as I got older, and I began feeling more guilty.

Disappointment never waited long. There was a big trip that the sixth graders went on every year. It was a week-long retreat to a local camp. You slept in bunk beds in cabins, had great meals in a dining hall and activities like archery, canoeing, and swimming. But no one in my house was going to be shelling out $150.00 for the privilege of me joining my classmates in this rite of passage from elementary school to junior high. So all my friends, classmates, and teachers went to camp, while I sat in the principal's office for a week. I was the only student who didn't go. Loneliness and sensations of worthlessness were becoming more prominent feelings in my life.

Everything about our household was always treated as top secret. Allen and I were never allowed to divulge too much information to anyone. We couldn't tell people where our parents worked, if they were working, what they did, who lived at our house, who had been to our house, when we ate, what we ate. All information was off limits. At the time, it seemed quite normal, and I assumed every family worked this way. It wasn't until adulthood that I realized most of these secrets were actually lies. The lies were told to keep me from asking too many questions. And if we did repeat them, we were the liars. My mother was a talented liar, and she was training me to follow her lead.

That vicious circle of lies and stories still haunt me. It is difficult for me to connect in real ways to those around me. Answering basic questions like "Where are you from?" can send me into a panic attack. And even after I manage to answer, it always feels like I'm talking about someone other than myself. That the stories aren't my own. I still worry that every story I tell may divulge something that will upset someone. Sometimes, I worry that I don't actually know what the truth is, like I'm living in a real-life *The Truman Show*, where you think one thing is your story, but in fact it could be all lies or completely made up. When you are used to not trusting anyone or anything around you, it's hard to believe in anything, including your own life.

As I got older I would lie in bed at night, contemplating. What had my parents done that had been so bad? What could be so unspeakable that I had to spend my entire childhood running from it? Nobody else at school seemed to be fearful of their own homes, with the exception of my brother and me. What made our family so different? And why. Why did I have these parents? Why did I have this life?

I was still dreaming of someone coming to my rescue, but no one ever did.

CHAPTER SIX
I THINK I MIGHT BE SINKING

"The scariest monsters are the ones
that lurk within our souls." —Unknown

IN RETROSPECT, I HAD NUMEROUS HINTS that my father wasn't really my father. There was a baby picture of me at three-and-a-half months old, one of the very few photos I had. On the back it said "Shenandoah Douty" in my mom's handwriting. *Douty? My name is Bradley.* I didn't ask about it, afraid mostly, but a seed had been planted.

The idea that my father wasn't my father seemed preposterous and I had refused to acknowledge the information. Until one day...

My brother and I were arguing over the volume of the television. It didn't take much for us to find something to bicker about. Allen, nearly 17, had not learned to gain control of his temper, and I knew how to push his buttons. My brother ended up grabbing me by the hair and dragging me around the living room. I screamed, "I'm telling Dad when he gets home!" Stating this simple sentence was usually the pressure point to get my brother to release his hold on me. He was scared of my dad. We both were.

Not today. Allen let go of my hair and proudly, like a peacock fanning its plume, announced, "He's not your dad. You don't even know your dad!" These words from my brother's mouth, this secret held for my entire life. I had been trapped in a delusion, a delusion that I was content believing in.

I felt a crazy sensation, like the compass of my world spinning uncontrollably. I was trying to calibrate to true north. I thought, *"He doesn't know what he's talking about. He just wants to win this argument.*" I wasn't willing or able to accept the truth.

When my mom came home later that day, I was relieved my father wasn't with her. I could tell she was in an unsettled mood, and normally I wouldn't dare be so brash with a question. But since the words had left his mouth, I just couldn't stop from thinking about what he said. I simply asked, "Is he my dad?"

"No!" She said it with such force and conviction, as if this was information that I already had. Maybe deep within me I had suspected it, but there would have been no indication my suspicions were true. This revelation sent me into a haze of confusion and astonishment. Without missing a beat, she added, "We are getting a divorce and moving out. You should start packing."

An explosion went off in my head. Not only was my father not my father, but also after a year of stability, the longest in my life, my mother had decided to divorce him. Just last month they had talked about becoming foster parents themselves, attempting to adopt a baby from someone related to my mother. I was absolutely dumbfounded by this turnaround.

My dad wasn't my dad, but my step-dad.

When he got home, I approached my stepfather about my discovery, in part to confirm the story my mother and brother told. I still couldn't accept the news, and I thought for sure he could put my mind at ease. "Well of course I'm your dad," he said. For an instant, I was washed over with relief. "You never met your other dad, and he never wanted to be a part of your life. So of course, I'm your dad." For him, being present meant that he was my dad, even if he wasn't my biological parent.

What about the story he had told me so many times, that he and my mom had conceived me in the Shenandoah Hotel? The story of how I had come to be? It was so convincing. Perhaps it had been another hint at the truth. I have a vague and foggy memory about a plane ride from California to Las Vegas. I don't know who put me on that plane, or exactly what was going on at the time. But putting the pieces together now, it appeared that my mother had already left California and met a new gentleman suitor in Las Vegas. I remember the plane ride, and sitting with an elderly couple. When we landed, I remember not wanting to leave their sides.

As the story goes, I got off the plane wearing a white and red frilly dress. I knew deep within me the story must be true. I had the sense that I hadn't belonged to my family this whole time. I even had thoughts of being kidnapped by these crazy people, raised away from my real family. And this news added to my confusion. I wasn't sure if it was proof of my kidnapping or confirmation of another fear, that I was doomed to this dysfunction, already thrown away by a parent who wasn't interested in me . Either way, I was feeling increasingly unsteady, and started withdrawing even further into isolation.

After this revelation, my parents split almost immediately and my mother and I started moving all over Michigan, to wherever we could find a space on a floor, an apartment of our own, or a man who was willing to put up with his girlfriend having a twelve-year-old daughter. My brother remained with my stepfather. He was turning eighteen soon, getting his settlement funds and almost done with high school. He helped my stepfather with his landscaping business, working after school and on the weekends.

I was too angry with my stepfather to stay. Angry for the lies, angry for all the pretending, and angry that all the punishments I'd received by his hand weren't from someone related to me. Escaping with my mom seemed like the solution to all of our problems. Finally, we would have the chance to do things right, without him, without his influence. Maybe this was the happy ever after my mother had been chasing.

My mother and I first moved into a house with a friend of hers, Darlene. Darlene lived near the junior high school that I would be attending that fall. My mother wasn't there very often, and spent much of her time with a new boyfriend that I hadn't been introduced to. That summer we moved at least four different times to various locations around town, both with and without the new boyfriend.

I had grown to despise my stepfather, and was feeling especially disgusted by him after learning the secret he and my mother had kept for so long. But Mom's new guy, Dewayne, wasn't any better; I found him completely revolting. He was 5'5" or 5'6" at the most. He had long, greasy black hair with bangs and an unnatural relationship with his nunchucks, constantly swinging them around his arms and legs. I'm not sure if it was meant to be intimidating or if he thought he was impressive. I found it nauseating. I hated being in the same room with him when people were around, and I found him intolerable when we were alone.

I wanted to hide from him, and started lying and making excuses to stay after school or work on homework that didn't exist. I went so far as making up a complete project for a report, which I completed, but never turned in, because it had never been requested by teachers. I didn't trust him, and unlike my mother's other boyfriends, who were easy going and fun, I thought he seemed sneaky and conniving. He seemed nothing like the other men my mom had dated and I was rapidly losing faith in her decision-making. I found myself looking for excuses to leave. Escape was the only thing I desired. Escape was always my fall back, and I desired it more than ever.

Part of this time we were living alone in a small, one-bedroom apartment. My room was actually a closet. It was so small that a twin mattress covered the entire floor. Utter desolation and depression had begun to overtake me. It became more difficult to escape into a book or a movie. Once, when my mom was off with her latest tryst, I thought it would be a good idea to try Jack Daniels straight from the bottle, to disappear as I had watched her do so many time before. I knew I wasn't supposed to drink and that the bottle was off limits, but I rationalized that, given the numerous times my mother let me have a sip of her beer or other drinks, this was no different. Besides, when was I going to have fun? I had been caged in the apartment for three days alone and I wasn't interested in watching *Top Gun* anymore.

I took a sip, and immediately began choking. The whiskey burned as is flowed down the back of my throat. Disgusting! I tried another sip, and the burning intensified. I spit it out in the sink. I put the lid back on, forced the bottle back into the cabinet and retreated to my mattress in the closet. I wasn't even good at drinking. Another failure to add to my growing list. It was a long time before I thought of trying alcohol again.

We moved back into Darlene's house for the start of seventh grade. We lived there less than a month, and I am not sure that I ever saw my mother during that period. I technically don't know whether I finished seventh grade. It was a grim time. I went to at least four different schools that year, enrolling in a fifth, but I never actually showed up for classes.

I was becoming disengaged with school and with the other students. In the past, I had pretended everything was fine. I would make up stories about the fun things I had done over the weekend, stories that I had copied from other kids at other schools. Trips to the movies, shopping, going out to eat, visits with family, all the things I heard them talking about. Recently, it had not been worth the hassle. I was tired of keeping track of the lies, and found it easier to just avoid conversation, choosing to disappear into the background. Schoolwork was becoming less of a priority. We had been assigned a project for the science fair, and I couldn't have been less interested. When another student, who seemed genuinely concerned, asked about my lack of progress I shrugged it off. I had completed too many projects for school in the past, only to be disheartened that I couldn't finish them. I knew we would be moving before the project was due. I was right.

The next move was into Dewayne's house. He lived with his mother and his two small children from a previous relationship. My disgust for him grew with each day. The house was filthy. I had been assigned my same mattress, but this time on the bedroom floor with his two small children. I hated living there so much that I would wake up and get ready for school an hour early, standing and waiting for the bus in the dark and cold to avoid contact with him and my mother.

Once, while at school, I slipped on some ice and hurt my ankle. Unwilling to go to the office for fear they would contact my mother, I managed to limp around until the end of the day. I was in terrible pain. After making it home, I showed my mom my ankle and she said, "You'll be fine." My ankle was swollen and purple. We didn't go to the doctor in my family, an expense that was deemed unnecessary. That night it was difficult to find a sleeping position where it didn't hurt. Eventually I fell asleep, but I woke in the middle of the night screaming from the pain. My mother came in and told me to quiet down. I never went to the hospital, instead I wrapped it in a bandage that I found in my mom's belongings. It took nearly three months before the pain subsided.

Near the end of the school year, I tried to move back in with my stepfather. It wasn't a decision that was easy for me. I had become bitter toward my mother for picking yet another man over my needs, especially one that I detested so much. From the outside it appeared that my step-dad was getting things together. He had continued to grow his business, and was living in the same house on Dale Street. I was desperate. And the devil I knew started feeling safer then the devil I didn't know.

My stepfather, who was now living with another woman and her two young children, agreed to let me move back. It was summer, and I rationalized that he could use my free labor at the business. However her two children now occupied my old room, so I was relegated to sleeping on an air mattress in the basement. It was unfinished, damp and cold. Over the years, my stepfather had erected several rooms out of the space, but the bare wood studs remained. Attached to one was the once-cherished autographed photo of Marvin Haggler, stuck to the door frame with a tack.

My air mattress lay on cold cement, the only thing protecting me from the elements and a truth I didn't want to face. I was alone again with very little hope of a normal family, a normal life. *Maybe this was normal?* And this man, a man who was still running from the law, a man who had dished out the worst punishments of my life, was the closest thing I had to a father and to a chance.

My mom's oldest sister, Kelly, had become aware of my situation. I'm not sure if my dad told her, or my brother, perhaps my grandmother, but out of nowhere she came for a visit. Excitedly I showed her my room, aware of the deplorable conditions, but not thinking what it would look like to outsiders. I was happier that I had a roof over my head, and Dewayne was out of my life. Shortly after, I had the opportunity to return to California to spend the summer with another of my mom's sisters, my Aunt Amy.

I spent the summer of 1988 with Aunt Amy in California. It changed my outlook and maybe even saved my life. I wished that it had never ended. I have vivid memories of that trip, one of the few fond things I like to recall from childhood. But, three highlights easily stand out. First, I was back in California, my favorite place. It was the place I called home. When I told people I was from there, they seemed impressed and jealous. I liked that. Second, I was with my cousin, Michelle, who was a year older. I quickly idolized her. She seemed like everything I wanted to be, and had everything I wanted to have. She was tall and beautiful, with long flowing blonde hair and lived in a magnificent home, with her mother and step-father who, at least from my perspective, seemed to love and care about her.

She seemed to have everything: clothes, cassette tapes, posters, spending money, and freedom. She did everything she wanted to and ate whatever she wanted. She seemed to have a very clear sense of who she was. I, on the other hand had no idea who I was. I had spent so much time lying and pretending that I had no idea who I was. Impersonating her seemed like a good start.

The third and most important memory I have of my visit with Aunt Amy was a feeling of safety and security. I never wanted to leave. Everything about being with the family made me feel safe and secure. There was a routine to their lives, and all seemed calm and easy.

In their house, schedules ran like they did on the TV shows that I watched and had longed to be a part of, like *Happy Days* and *The Brady Bunch*. There was a dinner with a set dinnertime, and a standard bedtime with lights out. Conversations included things like, "How was your day?" and, "What did you do today?" These things, the questions, which absolutely irritated Michelle and made her feel like her mom was being overprotective and overbearing, made me swoon with delight. *Somebody who cared about what I was thinking and doing? Someone who was thoughtful enough to put food on the table for me every day? Sign me up!*

The teen years bring angst, and I could tell that the relationship between my aunt and cousin had become a power struggle. Michelle didn't want to be in the same room as her mother. It was awkward for me, because what Michelle was going through paled in comparison to the neglect and abuse that I endured at the hands of my mother and stepfather. I would have traded places with her in an instant.

Her mom wanted to spend time with her. Her mom wanted to take her to the beauty salon. Her mom wanted to take her on trips to Disneyland. All these suggestions were rebuffed by Michelle, while I jumped at each opportunity. It was the first time I had been in a salon for a haircut, ever. I felt like a princess, and was thrilled someone wanted to spend time with me. I wouldn't say no. I couldn't say no.

I wasn't remotely afraid to spill my guts to Michelle. It was completely out of character for me, but Michelle was safe. *Who could she tell?* It felt great to get some of that anger off my chest. She barely spoke to her own mother, and in three weeks, I knew I would be out of there and likely never see her again. That's how I looked at it. Michelle became the first person I ever entrusted with some of my secrets, particularly how much I despised my life in general and my mother in particular.

Too soon, I had to board a plane and head back to reality. I replayed those few weeks over and over again in my mind for years. Perhaps I was only seeing what I wanted to see, but those memories and my interruptions got me through some tough and lonely days.

Unbeknownst to me, a completely different life awaited at the end of the plane ride home.

CHAPTER SEVEN
California Dreaming

"Hidden truths are unspoken lies." —*Unknown*

NOBODY WAS THERE to meet me at the airport when I arrived, which wasn't a complete surprise. Airline security wasn't what it is today, and I was able to convince the flight attendant that I would be fine. I would just take the city bus home. It was a small lie. I did ride the bus, but instead of going home, where ever that was, I headed directly to the small apartment where my grandmother lived in a nearby retirement community. I had stayed overnight with her before, and she always seemed pleased to see me. My couch surfing options were limited.

My grandmother was the closest thing I had to family or friends. With all the moves it was difficult to make friends, let alone keep them. When my mom and stepfather had a big fight, staying with my grandmother for a few hours made for a great free babysitter. My grandmother had a wanderer's soul, just like my mother. She was her own free spirit and lived on her own terms. She had five children and seemed close to none. She was an artist who had wandered the country, living in San Francisco, Costa Rica, and serving in the Peace Corps.

I don't know how she had money to live, but to me, she was ultra cool, with an undeniable appreciation of art and the liberal ideas that started at Haight-Ashbury and spread across the country in the 1960's. Both she and her twin sister were college educated. She could paint, read poetry, and was the only vegetarian I knew, a concept I hadn't heard of or considered before. She spent time with me, made me feel like I mattered to someone important. Her relationship with her children seemed odd, but I never asked. The past was an off-limit subject with everyone in my family.

My first real memory of my grandmother was when she came to visit us in Las Vegas. I was around four or five, and we had just moved from our trailer, to a barrack style home just down the road. It was small, and placed just a few steps behind the famous Las Vegas strip. Everyone seemed on edge, including my stepdad, who never liked having people over. He saw visitors as invaders.

The first night of her stay, she opened the window in the room we were sharing. I knew this transgression wouldn't go unnoticed. It was stifling, well over 100 degrees, and I thought the breeze felt nice. It lasted all of three minutes before my stepfather burst into the room, screaming that the air conditioner was on and that the windows couldn't be open. To this day I'm pretty sure we didn't have air conditioning. Even if we did, the air in the room was suffocating.

A heated argument ensued, and within the hour my grandmother packed her bags and left in the middle of the night. I wanted to crawl into her suitcase and run away with her. The tension between my her and my stepfather was palpable, and seemed to linger for an eternity.

I liked my grandmother even more because my stepfather did not.

When we lived in the same town in Michigan, my mother would visit my grandmother often, and without my stepfather. Grandma truly fascinated me. She could draw, sew, sculpt, and most importantly play board games. She taught me the ins and outs of games like Boggle, Scrabble, Crosswords, Word Search, Logic Puzzles, and all the other word games in her Dell Crossword books. She didn't take it easy on me, either. We would play round after round of Boggle, with me never winning. As we compared our word lists, my grandmother would say a word like "oleo."

"That's not a word," I protested.

"It is absolutely a word; grab the dictionary," she said, her crooked and wrinkled lips rising in a smirk. She appeared much older than she was. Her life experiences showed.

I reached for the dictionary, flipping the pages to the O words. Scanning my finger down each page, like I would across the atlas, I found the word. "Oleo, another term for margarine," I said with disgust. "Who would even know that word?"

"Me!" my grandmother said gleefully, almost singing. "And I bet you'll never forget it either."

She was absolutely right. I never forgot oleo, or the hundreds of other crazy words she taught me to win at any word game. That ability and skill now annoys my own family. When I was younger, I never understood why I didn't win when I played my grandmother. I thought I was terrible with words and games in general, adding them to the long list of failures and things for which I had no talent. Now I appreciate she was teaching me several invaluable lessons. Surely I would never have learned all those great words without her playing to her fullest capability. More importantly, she taught me that things don't always go your way, and that nobody in life gives you anything. You have to earn it. You have to make the choice that you want to earn it.

I stayed with my grandmother for over a week after arriving from California, with no word from my mother. Maybe my grandmother spoke to her, but if she did, she didn't let me know. I could tell that the rest of my mom's family, my grandmother and my mom's oldest sister, Kelly, were growing concerned, although nothing was said to me. I was never allowed to know the truth, about anything.

I wasn't worried. My mother had disappeared before, sometimes for a few days, sometimes for a week or longer. Usually I was the only one home, and I never told anyone. But this time was different and I could tell. My grandmother knew she couldn't continue to house me due to restrictions where she lived, so she called my Aunt Kelly, who had been a foster parent for my entire life. Kelly was always around. She was always rescuing my mom. She and my mother were very close; it's likely that they still are.

My brother Allen, who had turned eighteen by this time, had his inheritance from his father's death, and had purchased his own house. He wasn't interested in taking care of his 13-year-old half sister. I tried to wrangle myself back to my Aunt Amy's house in California, but it didn't work. "They can't take you on," I remember Kelly saying. I wondered if I had done something wrong when I was staying at Aunt Amy's to make her not want me, but my own mental safety nets kept that feeling from taking over.

It was decided that Aunt Kelly would contact the authorities.

And so began my life in foster care.

I was interviewed several times over the next few weeks. I never told anyone the full truth of what my life had been like with my mother, just enough. In my Child Protective Service[1] reports it simply stated:

> *Said child is without proper custody and guardianship, in that said child's home, by reason of neglect, is an unfit place for her to live in, in that in August 1989, mother, suddenly left the state without informing anyone of her plans, leaving the child behind. Shenandoah's former stepfather, who is presently the legal guardian[2], provided a home for her until approximately the end of December of 1989. Since the beginning of January 1990, Shenandoah has lived with an aunt and is currently residing with her grandmother, who cannot provide ongoing care. The mother has failed to maintain regular contact with said child and has not made any provisions for her financial support.*

> *Further, mother has a long-standing substance abuse problem and goes on drunken binges from which she does not return for days at a time. Her lifestyle has been highly unstable for*

---

1   My case began with a Preliminary Hearing in April of 1990. I was placed with my Aunt Kelly at the time. No visitation with my mother was allowed. Also, it should be noted that at the beginning the court does not have my legal name on paperwork. They later use my legal name, but then revert to using the first name I was reported under.

2   There is no indication that my stepfather was ever appointed as my legal guardian.

many years, characterized by frequent and sudden moves from one state to another and by neglect of her children's physical and emotional needs. Another child was abandoned when he was six months old.

The whereabouts of said child's father are unknown.[3]

While the authorities looked for a place to house me, my aunt said that she would take me for a few days, which turned into a few weeks. Then a few months.

My mom was always in contact with Aunt Kelly while I was growing up, and to hear my mother talk, it sounded like she had the perfect family. Everything always seemed too easy for them. My aunt had three biological children, and she adopted several others and fostered many, many others. Her kids were much older than me. At the time that I went to live with her, her oldest daughter, Lisa, had a baby with an abusive man. My aunt was the guardian for her grandson, and I think that she might have adopted him at some point. Lisa had another baby, but I never knew what happened to him.

I had little or no contact with my uncle. He was never around and my aunt took care of everything around the house. But it was very dysfunctional. No one ever touched, gave hugs or kisses, and I never heard anyone ever say they loved anyone else. We were all on a very tight schedule. We had specific shower times, teeth brushing times, etc. and my aunt's agenda was adhered to like a military drill. If you missed your time in the bathroom, you missed your time.

No one ever spoke to me about my changing adolescent body. I didn't know about things like deodorant, shaving, or feminine hygiene products until I heard other kids talking about them or using them in the school locker room. I had no one to ask, and didn't even know I should be asking. However, when I went to live with my Aunt

---

3   How could the court not put it together that my legal name was the same as my biological father? Court records never spelled his name properly, which probably resulted in him never being served with paperwork or found by his court-appointed attorney.

Kelly, she was fostering all boys in her house at the time. Everyone was uncomfortable with me being the only girl, but those boys had already become brothers to me.

Moving to my Aunt Kelly's house required a change of schools and a new environment. I had been raised in cities, but my aunt lived in a very small farming community on the western side of Michigan. It had one stoplight, and it blinked most of the time.

When I first went to live at my aunt's house, I enjoyed every minute. It felt as if I had won the lottery. There was a routine, a schedule, and meals at a real dining room table. I had been longing for just such a schedule; it made me feel connected. I had an influx of new "brothers," two foster boys who were in high school, and Aunt Kelly's grandson, who was getting ready to start kindergarten.

Then school started. I had been the new kid countless times before, and my aunt had introduced me to a girl in my class already, I wasn't concerned. That feeling lasted about 20 minutes before I realized that things might be a bit trickier this time.

I hadn't considered the fact that these kids had been going to school together their entire lives. Most of them had never left the town, or had only on occasion traveled into the nearby city to visit relatives or shop. They had their own routines, social groups, and were not looking for additions. It was also the start of eighth grade, and things like popularity, clothes and makeup were important to this group. While they had been important at other schools I attended, I'd never lasted long enough to be called out on it.

I had attended schools in the past where the popular or rich kids clearly had nice clothes, backpacks and accessories, but there was always a group that was willing to accept the new kid. Perhaps, as elementary-aged kids, there was less to compete over. But as a middle-school student, that seemed to change, and change quickly.

Everyone also knew I was a foster kid, because a foster kid from my aunt's house always came to that school. I went from being "the new kid" to the "foster kid" and I wasn't enjoying the label.

I felt like an outcast, and wasn't sure what to do.

Aunt Kelly knew everyone at the school, including teachers, coaches, other parents, and that began to make me feel claustrophobic. Now I lived with someone who knew my teachers. If I made a new friend, Kelly knew everything about her. It was an experience I'd never had before. I was used to autonomy. I was also used to keeping personal information to myself, so sharing the type of news you were supposed to share with a parental figure seemed like an invasion of privacy. It was awkward. And I started to feel like a guest in my own life story.

I had been living with my aunt for a month or so when my mother resurfaced, coming to see me at Aunt Kelly's house. Although my aunt didn't tell me that she had been in touch during this time, it was apparent, and I didn't like being kept in the dark. As I was growing older, I liked it less and less. While I usually enjoyed seeing my mother's smiling face again after an absence, my eyes wide like a child on Christmas morning, this time felt different. As we walked around the property together, and as I carefully listened to her latest escape plan, I became overwhelmed with a sense of grief, sadness, and remorse.

I knew as she spoke, almost instantly, that I would never see her again. I don't know why I felt that way, and to this day I can't explain it. Her plan was really no different than any of those that had come before. This plan was a move to Nebraska, a new job, a boyfriend, and yet another promise that things would be better. She would be better. But this time, after everything, I couldn't convince myself to jump on board. I couldn't give her another chance.

I stopped in my tracks and said, "Mom, I get it. I get that you're ready for a move. I just don't think I can do it anymore."

She stared straight ahead.

"I understand," is all she said.

Just like that, my relationship with my mother was over. No tears, no argument, no change in her plans. I refused and she merely gave up, went back into the house, got her purse, got into her car, and drove away. She was more worried about moving on with her plan than me.

As I had suspected, I never saw her again. I never really wanted to, at least not right away. In the months and years that followed, I would get nervous that she would change her mind and reappear. I would panic, because I didn't know if I would have the strength to tell her "no" again.

If she showed up at one of the ensuing court hearings and made a passionate plea that seemed sincere, the judge might be convinced — I might be convinced — that she had changed. Maybe I wanted to believe that she would show up. I think a part of me wanted to know that she loved me, even a little. As it turned out, I had nothing to worry about. I didn't hear from her for nearly five years.

During the following months that I lived with my aunt in foster care, my childhood was often a topic of conversation. My aunt had fostered numerous children whose circumstances had been worse, much worse than mine, so she tried to learn more, perhaps sensing that I wasn't telling the whole truth. Our conversations often felt like interrogations or insincere counseling sessions. She was a self-proclaimed psychologist, and believed that my mother was a manic-depressive. She might have been right, which likely meant for my aunt that I was, too. She built a strong case.

Sitting in her living room, heated by a wood stove in the corner and decorated with old farmhouse furniture, she calmly questioned me. "Do you feel guilty, worthless or helpless?" The other kids wandered around the house, meandering in and out of the conversation. As a foster kid you got good at hiding in the open, not wanting the conversation to drift into talk about you.

"Of course I do," I said. "I feel guilty that my mom is on her own. I feel helpless that there is nothing I can do for her."

"How about your mood, how would you describe it?" She seemed to have a list of the symptoms which I would later learn she was running down. Was I a manic depressive, or did I have bipolar? Clearly she believed I had an illness.

Each time, I unknowingly answered in the affirmative, one step closer to her diagnosis. Of course I felt sad or depressed, and yes, my thoughts continued one after another like a train. Each answer brought me closer to what everyone else already seemed to know. I was like my mother!

My depression, according to Aunt Kelly, didn't seem to be related to my situation. It wasn't because I was grieving the loss of my parents. It wasn't because I was enduring the crazy rules of foster care. That included no sleepovers at friend's houses, no school trips, having to get permission from the State of Michigan to participate in school activities and athletics. I wasn't allowed to be photographed or have a haircut without getting permission. The stress of court dates and looming unknowns certainly couldn't cause anxiety in anyone, especially a 13-year-old. Maybe my aunt was right. I was like my mother, and there was nothing I could do to change that.

CHAPTER EIGHT
IF YOU'RE CRAZY, DO YOU KNOW IT?

*"Insanity is relative. It depends on who has
who locked in what cage." —Ray Bradbury*

I WAS ANGRY. Angry and exasperated at everyone, especially my biological father. I reasoned with myself that since he had never attempted to see me in all these years — ever — he really wasn't my father at all.[4] I realize now that I didn't get that idea by myself. In fact, both my mother and stepfather had planted it there. They reinforced the idea so often during that year I found out the truth that I actually loathed the man. My mother, especially, took every opportunity to remind me that whatever she had done for me was more than my father ever had. It was a hard point to refute.

When I entered the foster care system, I was told by family members, my attorney and the court staff that my father was unreachable. Nobody knew where he was or how to contact him. This wasn't the first time I had heard this about my father. Every time his name came up it was the same story. His absence appeared to be a fact that everyone, including me, had accepted. It was during those times in court that I came to ultimately believe my father simply wanted nothing to do with me.

In the depths of my depression, torn on whether I wanted him to show up and rescue me or not, my mind would wander. I would imagine all the great men that my father could be. I took special interest in the fantastic stories on day-time television, like Maury

---

4   According to court documents including the original petition, my father's last name was misspelled and they had no address for him.

Povich, Phil Donahue, even Oprah Winfrey, about children separated from their parents at birth, only to be reunited as adults. It seemed that every great rock star was learning about a child they never knew they had, and I found myself wondering if one of them could be my father. They all had a storybook ending. As I daydreamed, I was hoping for one too.

On the one hand, by "choosing" foster care, I was admitting that what everyone said was true, my father didn't want me. I struggled with that. What if he wanted to be with me, he just didn't know how to find me? My mom had dragged me all over the country, and she certainly didn't want to be found. What if I had been kidnapped? What if she wasn't my real mother? With no social media and no internet, tracking someone down was far more difficult. So I wondered, was there something I could do? Should I try to track him down? Maybe if I was looking for him while he was looking for me, the chances of us finding each other would be doubled.

During the court proceedings, I listened and heard everything that everyone had to say about my mother and my father, all negative. There was testimony from caseworkers, attorneys, even my Aunt Kelly, about how they had no idea where my father was or how to contact him. My own experience had proven that he'd never been a part of my life. I had never met him. But something deep within me longed for a connection, a family connection to someone, anyone. I was desperate.

When I look back on my conversation with my mother that summer day in my aunt's yard, I have some regrets. I admit that when I made the decision to call it quits, it seemed like an easy way to get my storybook ending. Even though I was taught to distrust the system and to question authority, I had a fantasy that some loving couple that couldn't have children would want to adopt a middle-school student. I wanted a fairy tale conclusion. The one where you find out you were kidnapped and raised by the evil witch, only to be rescued and told you're really a princess.

But the truth is, as naïve as I was about the big, bad world, my mother made it hard to love her. The countless sleepless nights, the missed parent-teacher conferences and dance recitals, days when I was left home alone, days of finding her passed out in the bathroom, packing and leaving in the middle of the night, the garbage bag suitcases, the countless moves and countless losses. It made it hard to love anyone, even my own mother.

I had convinced myself that if I escaped into the foster care system, I would be with a family who wanted a child. It was an easy leap. I had already begun to make excuses for my mother. I knew that she had my brother and me at a very young age, and I knew that she, in her own way, was doing the best that she could. If I could find a family who really wanted kids, then I could have the fairy tale.

What I didn't count on were the endless feelings of loneliness and despair that would never dissipate, haunting me for nearly two decades, even after I left the system. I had an emptiness that would never leave, and a fear of abandonment that would turn me into a withdrawn person, unable to communicate feelings, unsure if I even had any. Slowly, I was being taken over by a sort of infection that started cutting me off from the world.

It turns out that the authorities, or maybe it was my aunt, had issues with me being a pubescent girl living in a foster home that consisted of high-school-aged foster boys. It didn't make sense to me then, and I still struggle to understand. I don't know the truth about why my aunt found me a new home, but she did. I spoke to her when I was in care, but mostly at the pressing of my foster sister. Going back to her house felt like stepping back into a history and past that I was trying to forget.

While I had a good relationship with my grandmother, my aunt did not. I don't know why, but they actively disliked each other. I never saw or spoke to my grandmother after leaving her house to go into care. I didn't learn of her passing until years later, working on my own genealogy, and found her death certificate online. There are lots of things I wanted to ask, lots of things I wanted to say, but I lost the chance.

The move from my aunt's was mostly welcome. I didn't know if I could take another year at that school, feeling like the outsider. An entire year at the same school had been a record for me. I already knew I wanted a change, and this seemed as good of an excuse as any. Another escape was always welcome. I had been at Aunt Kelly's for eighth grade and part of the following summer.

Do what you know. Run, move, escape.

I had been given a good sales pitch by my aunt and caseworker about a new foster family for me. This "forever" family had three children of their own, two daughters and a son. In age order, I fell in the middle. My aunt had known the family for some time, and they had regularly attended foster family meetings and events together. She believed that the family would be good for me. They would dedicate the time to go to school events, let me become involved in school activities, and provide a stable and nurturing environment. In the weeks leading up to my departure from my aunt's home, I daydreamed about my new family and how, after so many years and countless disappointments, I was finally going to get the home and parents I had always wanted.

The new home was over an hour drive from Aunt Kelly's, in an even smaller farming community than she had lived, in Southwestern Michigan. I began to get nervous as we drove. I didn't want to be a let down to my new family. I knew from conversations with my foster brothers that this could be my last chance at a family, and I didn't want to blow it. At fourteen, everything was riding on these strangers.

As we pulled into the driveway, the house immediately struck me. "Is this where they live?" I asked my aunt. It was eerily similar to the last house I had lived in with my mother and stepfather. The house was tan-colored, with brown trim. A dilapidated detached garage was awkwardly placed at the end of the broken and cracked concrete driveway. The Dale Street house had been brown with tan trim. They were of the same architectural design. The same concrete steps led up to the front doors of each of the houses, and each was unfit for the size of the family already living there. I tried to beat down the feelings in my gut. *"Everything is going to be fine, this is your happily ever after,"* I repeated to myself, over and over again.

As we entered the house, I was greeted by the awkward glances of my new siblings, including a foster son around seven. These glances were all too familiar; I experienced them each time a teacher introduced me to my new classmates. I set my garbage bag suitcase down, and was introduced to everyone. I tried to smile and didn't say much. One of the sisters showed me around. The house had a typical regional basement, very small and unfinished, where the washer and dryer were kept, damp and scary. It was similar to my stepfather's basement, where I had briefly stayed during part of seventh grade. That basement spooked me.

The main floor had two bedrooms, a bathroom, a small kitchen and living room. When I asked where I would be sleeping, I was shown a small staircase that led upstairs to the attic. Suddenly I went numb. I would be sharing the space with my two new foster sisters. The attic was finished, but the idea of sleeping there brought all sorts of stigmas. Stories that my foster brothers had shared about other homes they had lived in while in foster care began playing in my mind. It was also one large space, with three mattresses on the floor. I would be sleeping in an attic with two strangers, in the open and with no privacy. My fairy tale was rapidly becoming a nightmare.

I had thought all families, with the exception of mine, were "normal". They all seemed so traditional from the outside. Even when families on television tried to depict fighting, it seemed mild from what I had known, and in the end everyone did the right thing. The only way I thought I could get a happy ending was by rolling the dice with these complete strangers.

But that is a child's mind. Everyone is wonderful, kind and caring. I assumed that families or couples who were taking in foster kids would be top-notch. Surely someone who had gone through vigorous training, underwent state background checks, and had a caseworker checking in on them regularly would be the greatest parents of all.

What I hadn't realized or taken into account was that the system is broken. There are hundreds of thousands of kids in care, and very few options on where to place or even house them. Caseworkers change monthly, sometimes more frequently. I lost count of the number of caseworkers I had after receiving three different ones in the span of two months. Just when I thought I could trust one to share what was really happening in my life, a new one would take over. My fear of abandonment amplified with each change. Because the family who was chosen for me had three children of their own, and other foster kids, it was clear that I was not there for them to dote on me like the long-lost daughter they had always wanted.

I had one purpose I soon discovered, and that was to help pay the bills. I had become a paycheck. I'd seen this with my brother years before, but this was the first time I became the source of revenue.

From the outside, my foster family seemed like a typical middle-class family. They had a dad who worked for the phone company, and a stay-at-home mom. They went to church and knew their neighbors by name. In the beginning, they seemed to be interested in my life.

I was eager to please, happy to play any role. I learned that the best way to stay out of the spotlight was to stay quiet and do whatever I was asked to do. When I first went to live with them, I was preparing for my freshman year of high school. I had grandiose thoughts about high school and what I would experience there. I had seen plenty of movies about high school, and thought I had it all figured out. I could meet friends that I would have for the rest of my life, go to dances, prom and sleepovers. For me, this was the opportunity to change my life. This was my chance to be normal.

I quickly became friends with the middle and biological daughter, Claire. She was a feisty redhead, who dominated not only me but also the family in general. She knew how to get her way. Stubborn to a fault, when she set her mind to something she was going to do it or get it, period.

In my life, I was very accustomed with going along with what everyone else was doing. Not because I wanted to, or cared to, but because I so desperately wanted to have a friend and belong. I had watched my mother and stepfather, especially my stepfather, do this time and time again. I thought that was how you had a relationship, and I was willing to do whatever I had to to have those feelings. I pretended to be interested in the things that seemed important to other people. I thought that if I did whatever someone wanted, or listened to whatever music they liked, then I would be their friend and they would be mine. This left me vulnerable, and often the scapegoat for bad behavior.

That meant my friends were often controlling people who liked to have their way. I was the welcome doormat who would just go along, too scared to say anything. Typically, whenever I tried to stick up for myself I felt guilty, thinking I was a bad person for wanting something different. I was often ostracized for speaking out, and so I wouldn't. This was what my mother had done to me, and I fell for it every time. However, in being submissive I never shared anything true about myself, especially with friends and my foster sisters. I lied, making things up about my likes or dislikes to fit what I thought they wanted from me. Lying was easy for me, and usually I didn't even realize I wasn't telling the truth. It was as if I was an actress playing a role. Except the role I was playing was my actual life.

I was so wrapped up in trying to be whatever it is I thought they wanted that I had no idea what it was I wanted. I said "yes" to everything, and when anyone tried to ask about my past, I did what I had been taught to do: I lied. *No, I never think about my mom. No, I'm not depressed. Yes, I like that band. Yes, I want to help you.* I'd push any real feelings away and keep moving forward. *Don't rock the boat; you don't want to end up in another home. It could be worse. It always seems to be worse.*

When Claire got a job at a supermarket in a neighboring town so kids from school wouldn't see her, she thought I should get a job there, too. I did. When Claire wanted me to do something I did it, without question. I was too afraid to step out of line.

I started earning an income at the age of 14 bagging groceries, then stocking shelves, and then cashiering. The money I earned didn't go into a savings account, it went to my expenses. I paid for any extra-curricular activity that I was involved in, like volleyball. I even had to pay for going to a school dance. So, when I received a check from working at the store for $37, I signed it over to my foster mom. I gave her my check and she would give me cash back for a fee.

I didn't have many friends at school, acquaintances mostly. I hadn't told any of them that I was a foster kid. It was something I tried to conceal, afraid of judgment. Maybe they knew, maybe they didn't. But I was trying to keep it a secret, and like most secrets, it was eating away at me. Like the school I attended when living with my aunt, this was a small school. Most of the kids had known each other since kindergarten. After losing touch with Saralyn from the sixth grade, I'd never had another friend that close. It was becoming even harder for me the longer I stayed in one place. I was unable to camouflage myself. I loathed each day of school more and more. I wanted to fit in, but when I couldn't make friends, but I didn't know how and I had nowhere left to hide myself.

Life without my mom wasn't so bad. In fact, it was easier than I initially thought. My birthday came and went without much fanfare. Considering that my mother had missed both my ninth and eleventh birthdays when we were together, her missing another seemed normal. Thanksgiving and Christmas were spent with my foster family's celebrations, where I was always the outsider, or at least that's how I felt. I was okay, not great, but not bad. I had spent most holidays with my mom locked away in my room, waiting to return to school, so missing another without her didn't seem like a big deal. There were definitely low points in those first months. I suffered a deep, nagging desire, a yearning to feel like I belonged, like I was wanted in the world. As the months slipped into years that feeling disappeared, or perhaps I got better at burying them.

I told myself that I didn't deserve love. I absolutely felt that I deserved loneliness. Something was clearly wrong with me because I'd never truly been loved by anyone. It seemed my lot in life was to be alone, stranded on my own island, sailing in my own boat.

Another turning point in how I felt about my place in the world came during spring break of my junior year. I was seventeen, and driving my foster mother's car with my foster brother and his friend. We were driving to a nearby town to go to the movies. I was going to pick up my boyfriend, Kevin on the way. He had asked me out when he first got to our school, and we started dating. I wasn't really interested in him, but agreed because I wanted to fit in with what everyone else was doing. It was a very superficial relationship, but we went through the motions. The road we were traveling was curvy, with farmland on both sides and farmer's drainage ditches off the road. A farmer had recently been plowing his fields, going back and forth over the road dragging mud on his big tractor tires. When the wheels of the car hit the mud, we skidded, and as a new driver I was not able to regain traction. We veered down into the drainage ditch and the vehicle flipped six times.

It took a while before help arrived. My foster brother needed two stitches on his cheek. His friend, who had been thrown from the vehicle, broke his leg. My ribs were broken on both sides and I had punctured my lungs. I moved in and out of consciousness. I'd felt my skin being pierced, and tearing, and then I was out again.

I woke up days later, still hospitalized. It was painful to breathe. My whole chest was black underneath my gown. My foster family had come when I was first admitted, but when I woke up, I was alone. I was alone the next few weeks while I was in the hospital, with only an occasional check-in from my foster family. Not my aunt, not my boyfriend, not anyone from school. I had known I was alone in this world, but now I was face-to-face with the reality of the situation. No one cared if I lived or died. No one cared if I disappeared forever.

My heart was feeling the pressure of my burdens, the infection of my sorrow overtaking me.

Lying in the hospital bed, I wished each time I fell asleep that I would not wake up. It was the first time I remember feeling that way, but it wouldn't be the last.

When I watched hospital dramas on TV — *ER*, *Grey's Anatomy*, harking back all the way to *Marcus Welby M.D.* and *Emergency!* — I always saw caring hospital staff. Even if you had been abandoned the staff would cast a motherly or fatherly eye on you to cheer you up. Somehow, this hospital didn't act that way. The staff was surly, just there to get the job done. They didn't care if there was a seventeen-year-old girl injured in a car crash that never had any visitors. It felt as though some kind of judgment was being cast upon me. I was the foster kid, who clearly had done something so bad that no one could stand to be around her. I couldn't even stand to be around me.

Several days into my stay, and to my surprise, I received a card from my mother. It lay propped on the table next to me for days. I think I was both afraid to open it and angry that she bothered. I hadn't heard from her in nearly four, maybe five years. When I finally coaxed myself to open it, desperate to alleviate my pain, I read, "This could have turned out much better if you'd have died." It was painful to read, and it hit me hard. I knew that I had let my mother down. I always felt like I took the cowardly way out, that I should have stayed with her to help her, to save her from herself. But I didn't. In reality, I left her and worried only about myself.

I had committed the ultimate sin and broke the only rule I thought I knew about family. I left her, and now I had confirmation that the world would be better off without me.

It was the last time I would ever hear from her.

I had grown up rationalizing my mother's actions: *This is how people act. Just face it, it's a hard life.* But I was also becoming an adult, and questioning things. Was it me who didn't inspire others to love me, or was it the people around me who couldn't love and be empathetic? I ran through the possibilities, and usually tipped the scales in favor of thinking it was my fault.

When it came down to it, was it possible to be this unlucky? I thought my mom was unstable and a little crazy, a drug addict, so I got out of the situation. I left her and chose to try and save myself, a decision that I had started to doubt after reading her card. Then, both of my foster families proved unstable and unable to love me as well. I thought — *How is it possible that all the other people in my life are crazy?* The odds just didn't seem right. Clearly, *I* was the crazy one.

When it was time to go home from the hospital, my foster mom picked me up, and then drove us to the grocery store. I was still in enormous amounts of pain, so I sat in the car, waiting for two hours while she shopped. It seemed that picking me up from the hospital was one of many errands she had to run that day, and my return home was painfully slotted in with the rest of the necessities.

For several months . . . years, I struggled with depression, despair and emptiness. Everyone around me thought it was because of my family history, a genetic predisposition to being manic depressive that I had supposedly inherited from my mother. *So, this is what it feels like when crazy has you clasped in its grip.* Perhaps with each day I was becoming more like my mother. It was a destiny I was starting to accept.

Luck and stars can sometimes align, even when you don't realize it. I had landed in a forward-thinking school district, in this bedroom community near the world headquarters of Steelcase. It was a well-funded school, doing progressive things like blocking classes, and blending science, math and English departments together. All of the students were expected to go to college; every teacher talked about it. Although it had not been modeled to me through my biological or foster families, college seemed expected at school.

I had often thought of going to college as a small child, but as life unfolded it seemed an unlikely possibility. I had little support and got mixed messages. At some schools, teachers would tell me how talented or smart I was. At others, teachers pointed at me and said things like "Everyone here, maybe not you, goes to college." Apparently this teacher thought that foster kids should find jobs instead of planning on college. However, I was watching as classmates and other students were admitted to colleges who had far worse grades than me. I started to wonder, why couldn't I go? A stop in the counselor's office to get some information confirmed my doubts. "People like you don't go to college. They go to work, serving people like me."

At the time, my guidance counselor was confirming what everyone else had implied to me. Foster kids should feel lucky just to survive. They should feel lucky that people want to take them in and house them, and luckier still if they find and keep a job that allows them to pay their bills. College was for the privileged, not for people like me. I had been reminded of that on more than one occasion.

It seemed like my options were becoming few.

One of the bright spots for me at this school was my science teacher, Mrs. Ellison. Like Mr. Derby, she was not popular with most of the students. However, she took me under her wing. She asked about things I might want to do as a grown-up. Because of some shows I'd been watching on TV, I had begun a fascination with forensics, and this led my teacher and I to talk about a career with the FBI.

With Mrs. Ellison's help, I applied for and received an amazing scholarship to an FBI summer training program between my junior and senior year. For ten days, we stayed in dorms and went through a kind of boot camp and basic training regimen. We learned how to shoot, investigate a crime scene, rescue hostages, and even repel from buildings. It was an experience that gave me hope that I could have an exciting future. I was competing against kids from all over the country, and felt as though I was in my element. It turns out I was a good shot with a gun, and had a natural mind for problem solving. Apparently my life on the road gave me street smarts that the other kids didn't seem to have.

Just as soon as my dreams were being built up, they were dashed again. I was informed that because neither of my parents could be located, I would never pass the intensive background check. My parents made me a security risk, and that made me ineligible to join the FBI's training academy.

It was hard to go back to foster care after this brief respite from the depressing reality of my situation. I talked to Mrs. Ellison, who suggested that if I couldn't get into the FBI, perhaps I should think about studying criminal justice.

The teachers and counselors who refused to see a bright future for a foster kid didn't deter me. I wanted to go out of state, get as far away from Michigan as I could. I started to remember my dreams of studying marine biology, becoming the next Jacques Cousteau, floating around warm seas swimming with dolphins. I had been infatuated with the ocean since I was a child, and done most of my school reports on various aspects of the sea. I enjoyed the idea of the solitude the ocean could bring. I began living in the school's library, researching schools that offered programs in marine biology. I quickly found I could not afford to pay the application fees for most colleges, let alone figure out how I would physically get there. When I shared with others the idea of marine biology, most rebuffed it as a frivolous and impractical degree.

After class one day, Mrs. Ellison asked, "How about Michigan State?" She was an MSU alumnus, and offered to pay the $125 application fee on my behalf. I had heard a rumor that my tuition would be paid by the State of Michigan if I went to an in-state school. MSU didn't have a marine biology curriculum, but I thought it might be my only shot to go to college at all.

I knew that I had one chance to get accepted into college. Other kids in school were applying to ten colleges, with "safeties" and "reach" schools being designated. But I had one chance. It was becoming a Spartan or nothing.

As the school year marched on, my desperation to belong consumed my every thought. Nothing about me seemed to fit in. Square peg, round hole, I felt my edges getting worn down. I wanted to be loved; I yearned to be needed. Yet I had begun to completely shut myself off from the world. I was only comfortable in complete isolation.

My eighteenth birthday was looming, and that meant being sent into the world alone. The things I would be able to take with me from my foster care home were few. I owned nothing, except for several items of clothing and a stuffed rabbit.

It was during this time of complete insecurity that I began to think about tracking down my biological father.

Much to my surprise, I did.

CHAPTER NINE
O FATHER, WHERE ART THOU?

"Hope is a waking dream." —*Aristotle*

LOTS OF TEENS look forward to turning 18. It brings all the ideals of becoming an adult, living on your own and expanding your wings. When you turn the magical age of 18, as a foster child you are done. Out. On your own. No safety net. This is both beautiful and alarming. The beauty comes from thinking that you finally have freedom from the foster care system, getting to make your own decisions, not living under another stranger's roof. What most teens seek, including those in the system, is the perceived freedom of adulthood. For me, however, horror set in when I realized there was no one out in the real world who would support me. There was no back up plan, no assistance. No moving home if I couldn't find a job.

As my magic number loomed, the countdown clock to adulthood ticking each day in my head, I found myself thinking more and more about my father. My real father. I ached to belong to a family. Thinking about leaving the foster care system and going off to college and a career with no real family backing was intimidating, and getting ever-more difficult to confront.

Maybe my real father wasn't the monster that my mother, stepfather, aunt, grandmother and court system had made him out to be. I was in such a panic that I was willing to convince myself of just about anything. After all, they were hardly reliable sources, having lied to me on countless occasions about anything and everything. Maybe my real dad was a prince, someone famous, or a highly successful businessman who would relish the opportunity to take me under his protective wing.

Maybe he hadn't even known that I existed, and the fact that I did exist and wanted to see him was information that had been withheld from him. Anything seemed possible.

Maybe he really was a monster. After all, who would let their baby girl disappear into the world with an alcoholic manic-depressive mother, with no plan to see her again? Thinking about my father for too long made me exasperated. Yet, buried deep within me there was a twinge of optimism and anticipation.

I often debated myself about whether I should try and find him. *No one knows where he is. Even the court system can't find him. How on earth do you think you are going to find him?* The only thing I knew about my father was his name, Steve Douty. I didn't know his middle name, birth date, age, previous address. I had no idea if he was married, had other children or family. A first and last name that I had found misspelled in my foster care paperwork. No last known address, no last known state. One night, while laying in bed staring at the ceiling, I wondered what to do. I thought that if I stared long enough and hard enough, the answer might just appear. It never did.

Days on my countdown clock continued to tick away. My foster parents had agreed to allow me to stay past my eighteenth birthday, which fell in the middle of my senior year, if I was still going to school full time on course to graduate. That was at least a temporary solution, allowing me time to finish high school. But I was looking to connect with someone, anyone. I was growing desperate to really connect. I had acquaintances in my life. Friends were still hard for me to hold onto. I still had a boyfriend, but the connection remained superficial. I viewed having a boyfriend as another box for me to check off my to-do list for normality and happiness, another action that I thought others expected of me.

I had hoped initially that Kevin might fill the void. Instead, like all the others in my life, he made me realize how big the hole really was, and how deep my pain was. I tried to ignore the feelings, hiding from them instead. We never discussed anything of significance and I never shared with him that I was in foster care. He was someone who made it easy for me to forget about everything else. I never opened up to him about my hopes and dreams, or what my life was really like, mostly because I was terrified of being judged and rejected. Pretending had become so much easier.

The loneliness, the lack of meaning and direction in my life, was an ache so deep that it made it difficult to breathe, even after my lungs had healed.

Then, on a whim, I asked a question that changed everything. I went to visit my Aunt Kelly, mostly at the insistence of my foster sister Claire. When I went for the visit, I hadn't planned on saying much of anything. But secretly I was hoping she might have heard from my mother or another family member who might want to take pity on me.

While sitting around the same table where so many tears had been shared, the family gathering place where good news and bad news were always exchanged, I stared out the window into the yard where I had last seen my mother. Little seemed changed. When I found out one of my foster brothers had killed himself after a home visit, it was around that table. When somebody ran away, I learned about it at that table. So it made sense that around that table I began telling Aunt Kelly about my desire to find my father. My need to know and understand the truth had become all consuming. It was the first time I had ever admitted that out loud, to another human being. I was anxious and nervous that she and others would be angry, worried that they might try to talk me out of it. Worried that they might not help me. I was terrified of being judged, and most of all tormented by the idea that just by sharing the thought I would be cut loose from the only family I had.

In an instant, without even the slightest hesitation, she slid the phone across the table towards me and said, "Try information in Seattle, Washington." I was stunned. My mind began racing at a million miles per hour. *She knew where he lived? Why hadn't she ever said anything?* I hadn't expected it to be this easy, this fast. I was reeling. I was still trying to grasp the entirety of the situation. *Did I really want to find him?* I must have been staring blankly for a while, shocked. I could feel sweat pooling in my armpits, beads forming on my brow. "Well," I heard her say, "Are you going to call?" She pushed the phone book across the table with the blank expression of a seasoned poker player. At that moment, I realized she was calling my bluff.

When I rehearsed this conversation in my head it had gone much differently. I had expected resistance, or even an argument. I had hoped that maybe, if I could convince her, my aunt might help me hire a detective. But this? This I hadn't expected or prepared for. I opened the phone book and found the area code for Seattle. I picked up the receiver and slowly pushed the numbers, barely able to control the shaking in my hands.

"Do you have a number for Steve Douty?" I asked the operator, sheepishly.

"How do you spell the last name?"

"D-O-U-T-Y," I replied.

"Only thing we have with that spelling is a James Douty."

"Okay, thank you," I said as I hung up the phone. I was crushed. I guess I should have expected it. After all, it couldn't be as easy as just picking up the phone and dialing. What had I thought would happen?

"What did they say?" my aunt asked.

"They only had a James Douty listed," I said, sadly. I didn't know if I was upset with my aunt, or disappointed that my search was over so quickly.

"Oh," she said. "Jim is your father's brother. Call back and get the number. I'm sure he'll know where your father is, or how you can find him."

I was conflicted. I had questions, and lots of them. How in the world could my aunt have information like this and not share it before now? She knew my father's family? He had family? I didn't want to waste time thinking. Reaching down, I picked up the phone and redialed information without hesitation. This time I asked for James Douty, and was given his number. As I began to dial, my heart was racing, my head pounding. I hadn't even thought about what I was going to say. *What was I going to say?* Before I could think of anything a man answered.

"Hello?"

I was speechless. "Hello?" the voice said again.

"Yes, uh, yeah. Hello." I was stuttering. "My name is Shenandoah Douty. I am trying to find my father, Steve Douty, and well uh I... uh...thought you might be related to him." My armpits were now puddles, and I was beginning to feel nauseated.

"You must be kidding me," the voice answered. I was taken aback. I wasn't sure what to say. He continued, "I haven't spoken to Steve in years. He refuses to speak to me. I'm his father."

Shock — complete and utter shock — fell upon me. Had I really just called information and now, several minutes later, was I really speaking to my grandfather? I tried to compose myself. I had so many questions, thoughts, but I was struggling to string a sentence together. I asked, "Do you know how I could find him?"

"How long since you've seen him?" my grandfather asked.

"I have never met him," I responded.

"You've met him," he said. "I would try calling my oldest son, Jim. I'm pretty sure that they are in touch, and he knows how to get a hold of him." My grandfather gave me the necessary information so that I could call my Uncle Jim. As I was jotting down the number, my thoughts were muddled. *I had met my father? I had known him? He had known me?* My panic turned to worry and confusion. So many questions. So many lies. So many secrets now being uncovered. My grandfather and I had a brief conversation; I told him where I was living, and he asked if I would visit. While I didn't promise, I do regret that he died before I got a chance to connect with him and his family.

Armed with a second telephone number, I was one step closer to finding my father. My real father. My biological father. A man that I had known. My final chance at my storybook ending. My mind was off and racing. How many brothers and sisters did I have? Was my father remarried? Did I have cousins? What about a grandmother? What had happened to the relationship between my father and grandfather? Were they all looking for me? Where did they live? Where had they been?

Slowly, ever so slowly, I came to grips with the fact that speaking to my father was going to happen. I was crying, filled with apprehension and nervousness, but also relieved. If I could convince myself to pick up the phone one more time, I might actually talk to my father before the end of the day. I tried to quell the questions in my mind. First, I had to try and reach my newly discovered Uncle Jim. Hopefully, he would know more.

An uncle, I thought. *I wonder how many more relatives are out there?* A world that seemed cold, large and lonely mere hours ago was slowly, with each phone call, becoming warm and wondrous. As I dialed the number, it felt as though my heart was going to jump out of my chest. I was nervous, excited, worried, joyful, thankful, anxious, stressed. All of it, all at once.

"Hello?" a woman answered.

I paused, not sure what to do or what to say. "Yes, I am trying to reach Jim Douty."

"Who is this?" the woman demanded.

How to answer that? I paused again. "Ummmm….well…I'm not sure what to say. I don't know." My stutter was back. I'd already had a dry run at this with my grandfather, but I was still confused and hadn't fully processed that conversation. I didn't know what to say to a stranger who had no idea who I was. "My name is Shenandoah Douty, and —" The woman immediately cut me off.

"Shenandoah?" she questioned. The tone of her voice changed. Maybe she did know who I was.

"Yes," I replied, barely squeezing the sound from my throat.

"You've got to be kidding me." Her voice sounded full of disbelief and excitement. "I'm your Aunt Diane. Hold on a minute, let me get Jim. He isn't going to believe this." She said something else, but at that point I wasn't sure if she was talking to me or to herself. She seemed to be in more shock than I was.

"Okay," I managed to reply. As I sat there in silence, I wasn't sure if her response was good or bad. I was sweating profusely, and the waiting wasn't helping. It felt as though I was on hold for an eternity. *Maybe I should hang up?* I thought for a moment. Suddenly, a man's voice asked, "Shenandoah?"

"Yes," I replied quickly, shaken from my racing mind once again.

"Your dad isn't going to believe this. I can't believe this." The man began to fire questions at me, faster than I could answer. "Have you spoken to him? How did you get this number? Where are you? Where's your mother? How old are you now?" They seemed endless.

"No, I haven't spoken to him," I said. "That's why I'm calling. I found a James Douty through information…my grandfather…your father. He said that he hadn't spoken to my dad in years and that I should call you to find information about him. So he gave me your number. Do you know where he is?" I was growing anxious, and it seemed the most pressing question at the moment.

"I do. I just talked with him this morning."

I began to cry. The emotions of the last several hours, maybe the emotions of my entire lifetime, came flooding out all at once. *He knew where my dad was!* I could tell my uncle was fighting back tears as I heard him clear his throat. "Let me try and reach him and give him your number," he said, gently. "He's out working, and I don't know if he will answer right away."

I gave him my telephone number, and then we spent a few moments on the phone. I don't think either of us wanted to hang up, for fear we might lose each other again. Then he ended the conversation. "Let me call him; he's not going to believe it. It might take me a little while, so stay by the phone."

I had been waiting for a call from my dad my entire life, so I found it ironic that I was now being asked to sit by the phone by his brother. But as I hung up, still crying, I was excited. I couldn't completely wrap my head around what was happening. I'd spent most of my senior year trying to figure out how to begin searching, and within a couple of phone calls I'd found my grandfather and an uncle. It seemed unbelievable.

Was this a good thing — finding my father? I didn't know, but I was filled with hope. More hope than I'd felt in a long time. It seemed like something might finally change for me. As I sat at that long table in my aunt's home, which served not only as the dining room table but also as a makeshift office, my head was spinning, my stomach in knots. I had the same questions as before, but now uncertainty began setting in. What if my uncle couldn't find my dad right away? How long would I have to wait to know something? What if my father didn't want to speak with me? What if that was it? What if I never heard back?

My aunt was silent, except to look at me with a scowl and say, "This is what you wanted." I didn't know what she meant.

I think she could see I was struggling to process that I might actually have a dad, with a family to call my own. Maybe she thought about how she had withheld this information for so many years, from me and from the courts.

"Why don't you go for a walk around the yard to clear your head?" She often suggested this in times of stress. The same walk I had taken five years earlier with my mom. "Your Uncle Jim said it might take a while to track your dad down, and sitting here staring at the phone won't help. If he calls, I'll let you know."

Her suggestions seemed perfectly logical at the time, but looking back I think more was going on than I knew or understood. After all, if my aunt knew how to get a hold of my father or another member of his family, why hadn't she called him when I went into foster care?

Even if my father wasn't interested in raising me, maybe someone else in the family would have been willing to take me in.

It's a question I've pondered for years. Why would she keep me from a family I desperately needed? A family I desperately desired? Why didn't the courts take more interest in finding my father? I have since resigned myself to the fact that I will never know the truth and that it doesn't really matter. I have already walked that path, and nothing can ever change that fact.

CHAPTER TEN
Skittish in Seattle

"Don't let yesterday use up too much of today."
—*Will Rogers*

ON MY WALK, my head was whirling with questions, with accusations. Hope gave way to fear. *What if my father didn't want anything to do with me, just as my mother had told me? What if she wasn't lying? Then what? What options would I have?* I couldn't think of any. The agony, the waiting was killing me. Several hours passed with still no word from my uncle or my dad. I was beginning to have doubts that my father would ever call. Faith was turning to fear. Then, the phone rang.

Tears began falling before I even picked up the receiver, overwhelmed with emotions, I was able to squeeze out "Hello." I was trying my best to calm myself. I couldn't believe that I was speaking to my father. For more than an hour we breezed over the inevitable truth about my life, both past and present. We talked about how my mother had kept me continuously on the move, how I was now in foster care. He told me that he had remarried, but that he never had any other children. We exchanged contact information and made arrangements to speak again the next day. I was so overwhelmed by speaking to him that I could barely remember what he had said and what I told him.

My father and I spoke several times over the next few weeks. We talked on the phone, and he sent me several letters. He told me about his current life as a contractor, and I feigned that my current life was perfect, afraid, as I always was, that I was going to be a disappointment. So I continued pretending, just as I had done my entire life.

Shenandoah   *4-26-94*

The most beautiful name I've ever heard! Wow... Where to begin. I guess I start with what's happening now. Well, I am happily married to a wonderful woman, Carol. She treats me like a king, and I hope she feels the same. I love her a lot and we have come a long way together over the past ten years. We have a small house on 5 acres about 15 miles outside of Bremerton. But I have a big shop for me to play with my little projects in (Harley-Davidsons and old cars). Yeah, I am still a long-haired leaping gnome playing with motorcycles, I don't know if Marlene ever told ya about that part.

There are no kids between us... well except for our dog's (sic), they are just like kids, to us...

Hell, I don't even know if you knew that's what most people call me "Rowdy." It ain't easy living up to a name like "Rowdy Douty," but I wouldn't have it any other way!

Am I going to (sic) fast for ya? Or am I just excited about seeing you? Whatever...

Hey I just got an idea, (oh, oh) when I come back for your graduation, what say you about us driving back to Washington together, and that way we could talk all day and get to know each other? And if you don't like that we'll just fly back and jabberjaw in double time. I don't know if you'd like to bring your car or we can rent one, ah.. There's plenty of time for that...

There is so much to say I just keep jumping around. I feel so proud of you, getting a scholarship to college and all, I don't know where you got your brain's (sic), but I hope ya put em to good use. I wonder (there I go again) if you can transfer your scholarship to out here, wouldn't that be cool, see what happen's (sic) some time I just think out loud, and well you know....

What do your foster parents think bout all this? I hope they've helped you out, you sound so grown up. I just can't wait to see ya. Heres (sic) some pics, write back soon

Love ya Bunches xxxooooo 'Rowdy

It was signed, not with "Love, Dad" but Rowdy, his nickname!

Understandably, contacting my father sent my life into a tailspin over the next year. I was only five months from graduating high school, and thanks to my science teacher, I had been accepted to attend Michigan State University in the fall. However, for the first time in a long time, maybe the first time ever, I felt like I was finally becoming a part of something. I wondered if I could go to college out in the Northwest.

I had invited my dad to come out for my high school graduation, and he suggested that afterward I should come out to visit his place in Washington. Our plan was to drive back, just the two of us, and spend time forging a real bond, catching up on all the things we had missed. I thought it would be the perfect occasion to tell him the truth about everything. I would tell how my mom had left me, abandoned me, how my stepfather was abusive, how I hated foster care and felt unloved and unnoticed. But my foster parents put the kibosh on a cross-country road trip, insisting that I fly by myself instead.

They reasoned that it would be inappropriate to spend so much time alone with a virtual stranger, even if he was my biological father. I suppose that I could have ignored their advice; I was 18. But I had grown accustomed to not rocking the boat. I didn't want to make anyone any more upset than they already were. I was already feeling intense guilt for finding my father, and I didn't want to add to the disappointment of missing out on the road trip by upsetting them anymore than I was sure I already had. I had hoped, for a brief moment, that my dad would step up and insist that we take the road trip. He never did.

After months of planning and discussing, the time finally came when I would meet my father face-to-face. I had these feelings bubbling up in the pit of my stomach, excitement, stress and anxiety. I had an intense fear that he wouldn't be on the plane. I was setting myself up for another let down. After all, how many times had my mother made plans or promises that had fallen through? But when the flight landed and pulled up to the gate, it didn't take long before I saw him. He had long hair that he kept in a braided ponytail, along with a matching beard. He was tall and thin, dressed in Harley Davidson gear, wearing a cowboy hat and boots. He looked like a giant kid, but also intimidating to an 18-year-old. He looked like a tough biker guy who, if you saw him lingering outside a bar, might make you choose to go elsewhere. He is only 21 years older than me, so he would have been about 39. Meeting him in person was truly bizarre. There was my dad, a complete stranger.

While I was full of nerves, he seemed cool as a cucumber. We exchanged an awkward hug, as if meeting your long-lost daughter after not seeing her for 17 years was no big deal. *Maybe it wasn't a big deal for him.* I pushed the thought aside. It would have been easy for negativity to overtake me, but I didn't allow it. I wanted to be present in the moment, to just enjoy it for what it was.

As we left for dinner, I wondered how was I going to tell him about the last seventeen years of my life? How was I going to reconcile the account of my no-good, neglectful father who didn't give two damns about me with this laid-back, almost goofy biker who had just shown up in Michigan?

We ate at a place called the Beltline Bar, a Mexican dive bar that offered up the best Wet Burritos that far from the border. He ordered a beer. I paid. It was the beginning of a weird dynamic, like I was the adult and he was the kid.

It had also been arranged, perhaps as a cost-saving gesture, or perhaps as a rare hint of hospitality by my foster parents, that my dad would stay at their house.

Outside.

In a tent.

There wasn't room inside.

They did provide the tent. And a sleeping bag. At least they let him use the shower, and he could come inside during the day. This set-up made me really uncomfortable. Everything about it was awkward and disjointed.

He stayed for a few days. He was always trying to hug me to show affection. I hadn't had a whole lot of physical affection shown to me in my life, and certainly not in the past few years of foster care. I couldn't even remember the last time I had been hugged. Being touched felt uncomfortable and artificial.

Yet with graduation mere moments away, and the ability to finally escape an existence that felt void of feelings, I was beginning to have optimism for the future. A future could be with my father.

My graduation came and went. My foster parents threw a small party for me, mostly attended by their friends and family. Everyone was generous in giving me gifts and money, presumably thinking it would go towards my college expenses or giving me a start in life.

Instead, my foster parents kept most of the money to cover their expenses for the party. I was given enough to pay for the cost of my flight to and from Seattle. I was on my own.

My dad left. I was to meet him two weeks later at the Seattle airport. I was anxious and couldn't wait. I had given notice at my job, a box hardware store where I worked as a cashier, and was hopeful that I would never return to Michigan again, instead going to school out in Washington. My dad's family was in the area — lots of family. I went from having no family of my own to a gigantic clan, with aunts, uncles, cousins, and grandparents. It seemed unbelievable.

My foster parents said that the trip was not going to be good for me. They reasoned that my dad had never been a father before, and needed guidance on what to do. But he kept telling me: "I'm just mad at myself for not doing more." He seemed disappointed that he hadn't tried harder to find me. He regretted he had let my mother take custody, even though he knew she was "not right mentally." I didn't know how to process all this, half agreeing with him ("Of course you should have done more! I went through hell!") and half ready to forgive all and forge a new relationship and life with him.

I arrived in Seattle, the future bright.

I wanted him to be wonderful.

It turns out that anything short of the actual fairy tale ending I had in my head was going to be a let down. I had wanted my dad to stick up for me, for us, about us taking the road trip back out to Seattle, but he caved in to what my foster parents wanted. It was an extreme disappointment. Not taking that trip with him probably set our relationship back ten years.

Here's the reason: His wife. His wife had no interest in me. She appeared jealous that somebody had popped into her husband's life, a surprise she never expected or desired. She made it a point to let me know that she was not excited to have an 18-year-old kid on her doorstop, ruining her life.

She was fearful and aggressive. She worked to undermine my relationship with my father, and she succeeded. When we first started talking over the phone, I would call often, but she apparently never gave him the messages. I began thinking he didn't want to talk to me. *What had I done? Was I really that unlovable?*

It was an uncomfortable summer. Dad and his wife Carol lived outside of Seattle, across Puget Sound, on the Kitsap Peninsula in a remote area near Seabeck. He had several acres of land that were fenced and protected by his two Rottweilers. His home was a modest trailer, I only went inside on a few occasions. Outside were buildings for welding and other projects my dad was working on.

I stayed in my own camper some distance from the house, so as not to cramp Carol's lifestyle. It seemed normal. I figured that was how someone who just come out of nowhere should be treated. Carol barely spoke to me the entire summer. I had a few meals in the house, but otherwise ate mostly in my camper, heating food with the microwave. It was hot in the trailer, with no air conditioning. I listened to music on cassette tapes that I had hauled cross-country. I had been completely confident that I would not be returning to Michigan, so I had packed all of my belongings and brought them with me. My dad would come home from work, come out to the camper and have dinner with me, and we'd chat and talk. Occasionally one of my cousins would come over and we would go to the mall.

My dad took the ferry every day to his job. He was doing roofing and contracting work. On my first weekend in Seattle, he threw a big welcome home party for me. It turned out that I was the oldest cousin of the family. They had grown up hearing about me, but had never met me. I was a ghost. It was an overwhelming and paralyzing event. There were all these people, excited and happy to see me, yet I had no idea who any of them were.

I sat and chatted with my grandmother. It seemed like a fantasy. She asked about a stuffed toy she had made for me, and wondered if I remembered it. It took everything I had not to cry. *Love Bunny*? My friend and confidant? The one thing that had comforted me during my darkest times? I told her it was the only possession that remained from my childhood. She seemed happy that this gift of hers was so special to me.

I headed over to my camper to retrieve Love Bunny for her to see. I never left home without her, always making room for my still-treasured friend. On my way, Carol confronted me. "You need to get in the kitchen and do the dishes," she demanded. I was lost for words. I hadn't known that I needed to help with dishes.

"Okay," I said. "Can I just show Grandma the rabbit that she made me?" Before Carol could answer, my grandmother appeared at my side. Feistily, she told Carol that asking me to do dishes at my own party after all these years was ridiculous. I could feel the tension between the two of them, and it was clear that it had nothing to do with me.

"I don't mind," I said, trying to push my way into the conversation, trying to appease everyone.

"No!" my grandmother insisted. This was beginning to remind me of the power struggle between my stepfather and maternal grandmother. I liked grandmothers. Carol gave in.

My dad's version of my early childhood and his relationship with my mother was very different from my mother's side of the story. I didn't know whom to believe. I still don't.

My father said that I lived with him until I was almost two. He and my mother had me baptized by every religion in order to protect me. He had also taken care of my brother Allen from time to time. In fact, when I was around five, my brother had been living with him full time even though he was no relation. He had brought Allen to Las Vegas, where he was going to say goodbye to our mother and pick me up to come and live with him. When he returned from his hotel room to where my mom was staying, we had disappeared. He was never able to find us.

He told me how when my brother's father passed away, it was he that had flown with me, barely one at the time, to Michigan for the funeral. He explained how he had been in such a hurry that he'd left my diaper bag in the car. While on the plane, he had to borrow a bottle and diaper from another passenger.

Although he shared his story of my baby years, he never did what I was hoping he would do. I wanted him to apologize for not finding me and claiming me back from my mother. Maybe he didn't think he needed to, but it felt as though he didn't want to have me in his life. A baby, a child, a teenager, might have made it difficult for him to pursue his life's goal, to never have to grow up. Still, at some point during the summer, my dad asked me if I could transfer my acceptance to Washington State University. I was excited by the proposition. It was what I wanted.

When I called back to Michigan to feel out the possibility, I was greeted with the news that I could try and get accepted to Washington State, but that it wouldn't be paid. If I wanted to receive college tuition reimbursement from the State of Michigan, I had to attend school in Michigan. I was devastated. I shared the news with my father, who convinced me that going to school in Michigan, for free, was a better idea than paying for school in Washington. He promised that regardless of where I was, he would never lose me again.

I didn't want to go, but I left Washington, arriving back in Michigan two days before Welcome Week started at Michigan State University. I was disappointed that I wasn't able to stay with my dad and his family, but excited to start college as well. I thought that I would see my dad over the holidays, that we would have weekly father/daughter chats over the phone.

But it would be another seven years before I would see him again.

No birthday presents. No Christmas cards. No phone calls. I was forgotten, again.

CHAPTER ELEVEN
THIS PLACE IS DEATH

*"Intelligence without ambition is a bird
without wings." —Salvador Dali*

I HAD SURVIVED FOSTER CARE. Not unscathed, but I had survived. I had connected with my father and newfound family. I was back in Michigan, and as much as I didn't want to return, I was excited for the future. While my trip to Washington hadn't been the best my dad was in my life and anything still seemed possible.

I settled in at my residence hall at Michigan State University in East Lansing, Michigan. MSU is home of Big Ten football and a massive campus, with close to 50,000 students and 4,000 professors. Because of its setting, it was easy to get overwhelmed by the sheer size. My feelings of alienation were just below the surface when I arrived on campus. It didn't take long for them to begin to overtake me.

When I had applied to college, I thought it would be the answer to all my problems. I thought that at college, as an adult, making my own choices and developing my own friends, my chosen family, that I would find my place in this world. It was a place where nobody knew my story, where nobody had any judgments or preconceived notions about me. It was a place where I could be the person I wanted to be. Whoever that was.

I had a real fresh start. Creating my own persona and belief systems, not living under the shadow of my mother or the system. I thought college would give me the stability to have a career and a family, and that all I had to do was show up. I had spent so much of my childhood thinking about college, planning it as my escape, that somehow when the time finally came to go I assumed all the answers would unfold themselves, that things would magically get easier. Show up and, like in *The Wizard of Oz*, I would be shown what was behind the magic curtain.

Moving away and meeting new people didn't frighten me. I had done that many times in my life, and this was no different. I was excited about all the new opportunities and possibilities I had and the chances I got. I felt focused in the first month of college, ready to get good grades and to succeed in life.

College was supposed to be the best years of your life. Everyone said so.

But as much as I wanted to leave my past behind, the legacy of foster care meant that I had no family support or source of income. There were no checks coming in to pay for my expenses.

I had zero financial literacy and now that I was legally an adult that was dangerous. I had no idea what a checking account was. Paying bills, even understanding what bills I was receiving and why, balancing a bank account, I had no idea how any of it worked. When I received a refund check for one of my grants, it sat on my desk for a while until my roommate saw it. "What are you doing with this?" she asked. I explained that I had received it, but didn't know what to do with it. She took me to the campus bank and helped me open up an account.

I had no clue how to turn the check into cash, because my foster mother had always taken my checks and given me cash in return. But when I asked, the staff at the banks and credit card companies responded positively. They gave me a checking account. Then they gave me a credit card. I didn't take advantage of my line of credit. At first.

I had thought, initially, that I would keep in touch with my foster family. They weren't my favorite people, but we did have a familiarity with each other, and they had taken me into their home and provided me with food and shelter and reliability. There was far less drama in that house compared to living with my mother, a constant reminder that it could always be worse.

I had been in college less than a month when I received a phone call from Claire. She relayed that my foster mom needed to borrow money to pay the bills. My foster parents always needed money. This was a constant source of conversation and worry in their house. I indicated that I only had $64 left from my paycheck from the campus jobs I had taken on to help make ends meet. I was instructed by Claire to take out a credit card, get a cash advance for as much as possible, and send it to them.

I didn't question or hesitate to do as she instructed. I didn't understand bank accounts. I had no idea that credit reports and credit scores existed until much later. In fact, I even missed class to get the task completed. I went to the local bank for students, and took out a cash advance for $5,000. Then I walked across campus and mailed a money order from the Student Union.

Three days later, I received a threatening call.

"Shen, did you actually mail the check?" asked a voice.

I knew immediately that it was Claire. "Of course I did," I said.

"You're sure?" she continued.

"Yes, I mailed it from the Student Union three days ago."

"Well, it hasn't arrived, and like I told you, Mom needs that money immediately," she scolded.

"I mailed it." Before I could finish, there was nothing but a dial tone. There was no inquiry into how I was doing, whether I'd made any friends, what life was like on campus.

I played back my every step in receiving and mailing the check to be sure I had done it properly. Yes, I had mailed it. I was sure I put the right address on the envelope. I hated feeling like a disappointment, but I wasn't sure what else I could do.

I was struggling as a college student, financially and mentally. I was working and going to school, trying to better myself, and the only thing my foster family were concerned about was that I hadn't mailed them money. I received a similar call from Claire every day for five days, each one growing more desperate and aggressive.

Finally the calls stopped for two days. On the eighth day I received a message on my dorm phone that the check finally came, though it had been damaged in the mail. I received no apology. It was the last time I spoke with anyone from that family. The money was never paid back.

Three weeks later, when the bill arrived, I learned that I owed $5,000 to the bank. I had no idea how I could make the payment, even the minimum payment. Shortly after, I discovered that I wasn't getting a free ride to MSU, as my foster parents had implied. I knew I was given an on-campus job to pay my part, but I didn't realize I had to do that and pay for college as well. There was tuition to pay, and room and board. The total equaled around $10,500 per year. Now that I was stuck in Michigan I realized that I could have moved to Washington after all, and been with my father and his family.

But now I was stranded. I had no money, no hope, and no escape.

This crippling news didn't help my social life. I had already given up trying to become involved with on-campus activities, simply because I couldn't afford to. I was constantly thinking about work and how to make more money, often trying to pick up additional shifts, which usually meant working Friday and Saturday nights. There was little time for me to socialize. I was starting to accept the fact that I was the crazy one, and little by little it felt that I was turning more depressive and more like my mother. My roommate never did warm up to me, or maybe I never warmed up to her. After all, I didn't have a great track record when it came to making or keeping friends. I got invited to parties, but was completely uncomfortable; I had no idea how to fit in. Maybe I didn't want to fit in.

After about three months, the Resident Advisor on my floor suggested, "Maybe you should go somewhere else?" I spoke to housing staff, and was successful in getting transferred to a dorm with three to a room, with roommates who had lived together the year before and were looking to save a little money.

I was stringing together different part-time jobs, working 25-30 hours a week. I worked on campus, helping professors with various research projects. At the computer lab before campus e-mail, I sat at the Help Desk. I made less than $3 an hour.

I was becoming completely isolated socially, emotionally and mentally. I didn't feel connected with the other students or the classes I was attending. I was becoming disenfranchised with things I thought would be fixed by enrolling in college in the first place. The feelings I had in high school that I thought would vanish in college — the feeling of not belonging — seemed only to be growing more intense.

I found myself sinking deeper and deeper into a depression. The mental baggage of my past was colliding head-on with the present, and I felt there was nothing I could do to stop. My escape route to the good life had come to a dead end. I recognized that I had a complete inability to engage with people on anything more than a superficial level. While I was able to start a conversation, laugh, and enjoy a good story, I was unable to maintain the interaction in a meaningful way. I would meet a student or teacher on campus and initially carry on a discussion, have meals together, maybe even go out to a party or other social event. This would last a month or so, and then I would find myself bored and completely disinterested. The other person had done nothing wrong. I just lost the ability to enjoy his or her company, and saw no reason to maintain the relationship. It was time to move on, like I had done so many times before. Staying connected for any length of time was a struggle for me. I absolutely did not know how to be a friend, or what having a true friend was even like.

It was easier for me to withdraw into my own world, especially on such a large campus.

When I was at my lowest, unable to find the light at the end of the tunnel, I had the realization that I didn't have to go to class if I was feeling tired or depressed. No one was going to find out. No one was going to make me. No one was telling me what to do anymore. No one cared. My grades plummeted.

I was on the verge of being kicked out.

Letters and cards that my dad had been sending stopped. I was unable to call or write, because I couldn't afford to. It was clear that I didn't know how to have a relationship with him, or with anyone else for that matter. If the other person couldn't do their part plus some, I was of no help. I was failing at taking care of myself.

Every night I convinced myself that, with all the terrible things that had happened to me in my life, it was time that I was spared more grief, angst or anguish. I hoped that my life would come to an end.

When morning came, I awoke disappointed that I had survived the night to the reality of a new day. It was as if I had an open sore that was festering. After nearly three months I decided that if God wasn't going to do it for me, then I would do it for myself. I had prescription medication left from my wisdom teeth being pulled a few weeks prior. I thought I could overdose. It would be an easy and painless way to go.

I took maybe six or seven pills, everything that was left in the bottle, and laid down to go to sleep forever. I felt comfortable with my decision and at peace with myself, and for the first time in a long time, I felt free. I closed my eyes.

My roommate came home and noticed me. She began calling my name, and I was awakened by her pushing on my arm. "Shen, how long have you been sleeping?" she said.

"What? What time is it?" I felt very groggy.

"It's 3:00 p.m."

"It can't be 3:00 p.m.," I said. "I laid down at 6:00 p.m."

"I didn't come home last night," she said. "Why did you go to bed so early?"

I sat straight up in my bed, almost forgetting that I had tried to commit suicide. "What day is it?"

"It's Sunday. Why would you go to bed at 6:00 p.m. on a Saturday night?" she asked. My roommate had become quite the socialite while in school. Growing up in a strict family, she had decided that her unsupervised college time was a great place to become the next cover model of Girls Gone Wild.

"Sunday? I went to bed on Friday at 6:00 p.m.," I said. As soon as I said it, I knew I had better come up with an excuse. "I think I'm coming down with something. Maybe I should go see the campus doctor."

"Sounds like it. Who sleeps for two days without drinking?"

Disaster averted. She had no idea what I had attempted, and I was left feeling more disappointed than ever.

My birthday came with no one noticing. Several weeks later, Christmas and New Years passed without much celebration or fanfare. The campus was virtually empty. I had moved temporarily into the International Hall for the holidays, and the people there were graduate students and those who couldn't make it home for the holidays. My depression was worsening, and having the energy or desire to go to class was becoming rarer.

Luckily, another caring teacher reached out. He was questioned why I was showing up late and missing our scheduled meetings. I confided to him that I thought I was a manic-depressive, and I feared that I was going crazy. I was desperate. I think I wanted answers to why I was feeling this way. I felt very empty. I think I would have been happy with anything he said, just to have an answer. He was clearly not in agreement with my assessment, and referred me to a colleague — an expert in the field — for help. At the end of our second session, the psychologist looked at me and said simply, "You're not crazy, and you're not manic depressive."

These words hit me like a thunderbolt.

"I'm not?" I asked sheepishly.

"No. In fact, given your circumstances, some might categorize you as a miracle."

The answer I got wasn't what I was expecting, leaving me even more confused.

I realized that, throughout my entire life, I had been put into one box or another, labeled one thing or another. I understood that the adults around me knew it was easier to control me if they labeled me; I had seen it numerous times with the other kids in the system.

As soon as someone told them how bad and screwed up they were, they would simply live up to that appraisal. I observed it with the older boys in my aunt's house countless times. When I first arrived in her home, they would confide their hopes and aspirations about life after care, where they would go, the things they would do. But little by little, with each visit from the social worker, those dreams would erode. Soon they were reduced to just hoping for a job that would allow them to survive. Some of them did go on to live unassisted lives, but most succumbed to what the system deemed their prede-termined fates: addiction, criminal records, and in some cases, death.

After my meeting with the psychologist, I swore that I would never allow someone to label me again. Instead, I would live my own life, the way I wanted to live it. I would take the power, and I would never allow someone to tell me who and what I was ever again.

This was an invaluable lesson. At various times in my life I've lost touch with that vow, but I always come back to it, again and again. It's all about individual choices. We all make choices every single day, and it's my choice if I want to believe the naysayers. It is my choice to get out of bed. It is my choice to be miserable. So many people have tried to categorize my mother, too. Was she sick? Was she a drug addict? Was she abused? Was she mentally ill? Again and again, my answer is the same: "I don't know." I know how painful it was for me to be placed into a box and categorized. I later learned it was common practice — and had value, both in power and profit — for those who did the categorizing. But I won't do it, even to my mother. I have no time for judgment.

I was briefly euphoric. I wasn't turning into my vagabond, drug-ad-dicted mother. I felt genuine relief. Yet there was a nagging sensa-tion in the back of my mind. *Now what?* My circumstances hadn't changed. I was still alone on a crowded campus, working crazy hours with huge bills to pay. I had no friends, no family, not even a case-worker to check in on me. No safety net. I could have gone missing and people might not even know or care. In a way, I almost wished that there *was* something wrong with me, because then I'd be seeing a counselor who would be charged with looking after me. At least it would be someone I could trust.

I was in a quandary that this life and the responsibility for making it work was mine alone. I couldn't blame my failures on faulty wiring in my brain. I couldn't blame them on the way I'd been raised. Sure, I was friendless, and penniless, but I was an adult. I had to find a way to make it work.

CHAPTER TWELVE
FROM SURVIVING TO THRIVING

"When you get to the end of the rope, tie a knot
and hang on." —Thomas Jefferson

I STARTED TO TAKE ACTION. I sold my textbooks back to the bookstore and I sold my blood plasma so I could eat. I even briefly considered, could I be a topless dancer? Or sell the eggs in my ovaries? Maybe that was taking it too far. But, when you are hungry and don't have enough money to afford your next meal, let alone pay your bills, you consider a lot of desperate measures. No idea was ever completely off the table. In these situations, you see how easy it is to prey on people who are up against the wall, with few options.

The amount of money I was making on campus was not enough to survive. Undaunted, I found a full-time job entering in orders for a wholesale art supply company just off campus in Lansing. Now I was working between thirty and forty hours a week, while still trying to go to school.

By May of my freshman year, my dorm was closing for the summer. I hadn't been in contact with my foster family since the credit card debacle, and I wasn't communicating with Aunt Kelly. We hadn't spoken since she had helped me locate my father. Perhaps she felt as if my desire to find him was a betrayal.

Regardless, I was on my own. I had a full-time job that I desperately needed, so moving out of town wasn't an option anyway. I rented a studio apartment off of campus, and bought a beat-up, 1986 Ford Escort with 120,000 miles on it so I could drive myself to work. I also continued school through summer, hoping that I could finish college early. Unfortunately I kept failing the introduction to math class, which was taught by a Teacher's Assistant. His English was incomprehensible to me, so I began hunting for alternate solutions. I was looking for every possible way to save even $1.00, when someone at work mentioned that I might look into transferable credits from Lansing Community College.

Living in an apartment, I now had more bills to pay including rent, electric, gas for my car. I had to have the basics of furnishings, bed, plates, and cooking utensils. I couldn't afford car insurance, so I prayed I never got into an accident. I got a ticket because I couldn't afford to pay the state tag. I didn't know I needed one. If my car required anything, a new tire or repair work, it was simply not possible.

I remember trying to save money to buy my first cooking pan. The cheapest one I could find was $12. It seemed outrageously expensive. I didn't have $12. So I went without the pan for several weeks. Finally, after nearly a month, I had saved $6. I went back to the store and looked some more. I had decided that a saucepan would be the best purchase; I could use it to boil water for noodles, as well as to cook meat or other things. I took the pan to the layaway department, paid the $6, and made payments on the other $6 over the course of a month. It took me two months to buy a $12 pan. It was one of the only things I owned.

I saved for towels next.

One day, while waiting for class at the community college, I was scanning the job board and saw an ad for a receptionist at a law office. The pay was better than I was making, and I figured the office would be much nicer than the warehouse I was working in. I would have sold my soul for an extra 50 cents an hour. I went to the law office on my lunch break and interviewed with the owner, a woman in her forties. She could have been one of my mother's sisters. The office was small, and smelled of the cigarettes that she continually smoked.

In the waiting area, I sat at a small desk, which I'm sure she put together herself. From the ceiling hung at least 100 wind chimes, and gargoyles were displayed everywhere. It was far from what I had expected a lawyer's office to be like. No scales of justice or framed replicas of the constitution, very few law books. Instead there was a collection of bathroom jokes in the waiting room for prospective clients to read.

None of this shocked me. I had learned to accept the crazy in my life long ago. For me, it was more about the money the job paid than what my co-workers were like. Her idea for the interview was to have me sit down and do the job. She said it was the only true way to know if I was qualified. The phone rang. I answered it. I typed short letters and took messages for the rest of the day. I guess she was satisfied, because I was hired.

When I started, I had no idea what I was doing. My boss showed me a transcription machine with a stack of dictation tapes that needed to be translated and typed. I had never seen a transcription machine before, but without hesitation I put in the first tape and started typing what I heard, even though I barely knew how to type. When I couldn't get my stacks done at work, I took them home to work on at the campus library. She never knew. Every day I threw myself into the work, looking over everything to make sure it was perfect before handing it in.

Work became a place where I received praise, and where no one ever asked questions about my life or past. Maybe it was luck, or maybe she just didn't care, but my boss never asked about my family or friends. Over time, I learned about her. She had two children, and was divorced. She seemed solitary, like me, without many friends. She poured herself into her work, and often seemed in over her head. She was demanding, miserly, and surly. She reminded me a lot of my mother.

My hard work paid off. Soon I took on a larger role at her office, and started hiring and managing the student law clerks who needed to log hours with a working attorney to earn credit to graduate law school. I also started taking on tasks for the other attorneys who were renting single room office space from her. As time went on, I worked even more hours, 45 to 50 hours weekly. I wasn't getting paid for all the hours, but the more I worked, the less I was reminded of how alone I was in the world.

Now that I was living off campus, I didn't have options for the holidays. Another year had passed and I still had no friends. No relatives wanted me. Communication with my father was nonexistent. Initially, I had wanted to spend those first holidays after our reunification with him, but the cost of flying was too expensive for me, and he hadn't offered to pay for my ticket.

My aunt had continued to be absent from my life. Meeting my dad was the beginning of the end of my relationship with her. Maybe because I was angry that she knew where my father was for all those years, and never told me? Maybe she thought that I was being selfish in seeking out my father, and felt insecure that my new family was going to be better. We still haven't spoken. I suspect we never will.

Communication was something that I wasn't very good at, or at least it didn't seem like I was good. I was failing at every relationship in my life. I had failed at being a daughter, failed at being a sister. Failed at being a friend. The only person I knew how to reach was my stepfather. So, in October of 1995, I picked up the phone and dialed his number to wish him a happy birthday. It had been almost six years since we had spoken. He answered, and seemed both shocked and pleased to hear from me. It was the first friendly voice I'd heard in some time. We made plans for me to come visit him in Muskegon for Thanksgiving. He was still living in the same house.

I just wanted to be loved by somebody and eat a Thanksgiving meal with family. Even if it meant opening myself back up to the drama and abuse that came along with my stepfather, at least I wouldn't be alone, and I knew what to expect from him. I had been alone for so long that abuse felt better than loneliness ever could.

I left my apartment in East Lansing and drove the couple of hours to see him. He was living on his own, and had been forced into sobriety after being diagnosed with myasthenia gravis, a chronic autoimmune neuromuscular disease characterized by varying degrees of weakness of the voluntary muscles of the body. He was on a medication that didn't make him feel well, and he probably didn't think he had too much longer to live. I didn't mention finding my real father, and he didn't ask about my experience in foster care. We had a nice Thanksgiving, cooking the dinner and hanging out together. Perhaps we were both too lonely to talk about the past.

The one odd note that didn't strike me as odd until much later in life was that he wondered if I could introduce him to anybody I met through work at the lawyer's office. He suggested that somebody who had been a victim of domestic violence might be a good fit for him. After all, he wasn't going to beat them, so they would be grateful for a nice guy like him. That seemed to me like a perfectly normal request at the time. Now, I realize how deceitful and predatory he really was.

Christmas came around, and I was desperate to have a tree. I went to a tree lot and forked over my hard-earned money, money set aside for my electric bill, for a medium-sized fir that would fit in my apartment. I strapped the tree to the hood of my car, drove it home, and dragged it up to my apartment, where I propped it against the wall. I didn't have a stand or tree holder. That tree was all I had. I wanted to be with people, but there was no one for me to be with. I didn't have the courage to call my stepfather again, so I spent another Christmas alone.

After the holidays were over, I got back to work, mastering the transcription machine and the other basic office tasks. Soon, the boss had me doing more work I was not qualified to handle. She was having me read case law and make summary sheets by hand. I had no background in law, but was able to figure out what it meant to be the plaintiff and the defendant. At the time, I didn't have a television, so these briefs became my entertainment. I took them home, using my dictionary to help me understand the legal jargon, and worked my way through piles of them each night.

My boss was taking on free law clerks and giving them these types of assignments for the cases she had. She paid per project to have her cases researched. But, if she had already figured out a solution before the clerk turned it in, they didn't get paid. Of course, she fudged this policy quite a lot by keeping and using the research the clerks had done while claiming that she figured it all out herself.

She didn't like to pay full price for anything. I continued to be asked to perform legal work on cases that bordered on practicing law without a license. But I needed the job, so I couldn't complain. I went on process serving assignments where I had to serve people with legal papers including divorce proceedings, witness subpoenas and general lawsuits. I didn't know it was dangerous, and was naïve as I wandered into inner city Lansing, serving documents to all sorts of people and calling individuals to be witnesses in cases where they didn't want to be witnesses.

People are rarely happy to see a process server. Sometimes they yell, swear, and slam doors, and occasionally attempt to get physical. I did what I had to do. After a full day of answering phones, typing letters and being a para-lawyer, why not take to the streets of inner city Lansing to serve papers?

Clients and clerks came and went, until one day a clerk answered an ad to conduct legal research for the firm on a case-by-case basis. As always, I performed the interview. His name was Gerald, and he seemed like a nice guy. On his first project he figured out my boss was conning. When he arrived to turn in his first research project to her, and she refused to pay, he refused to give her his work. I was laughing in my outer office as I heard the scene unfold, and was glad finally someone stood up to her. While everyone else was groveling, living in terror of her, Gerry didn't care what she thought. I respected him.

It was clear that she would never ask him to do work again, but I didn't care. I could give him other assignments from the other attorneys in the office. I asked him whether he wanted to go with me to serve a process together. The law clerks and I would occasionally hang out together. I often tried to talk one of them into going with me as a back-up. He agreed, and the entire time he made jokes about how ridiculous it was that I was serving these papers. So, I wasn't shocked when he asked me to a movie, *The Devil's Advocate*, ironically about an up-and-coming defense attorney. When we got to the theater, I said something about the two of us being friends, and he said, "I don't want to be your friend, I have enough friends already."

We've been together every day since.

Eventually, after almost two years working there, I left the law office and went to work at a larger and more respectable law firm. I made triple the amount of money that my boss had been paying me, and felt the prestige of working for real lawyers. No more gargoyles, dirty joke books, wind chimes, or smoking in the office.

Working in the law, I saw what happened to people who couldn't keep up with the demands of their lives. We defended husbands who hit their wives, drunk drivers, thieves, and even 19-year-old kids selling crack in inner city Lansing.

I worked classes in around my work schedule. I took classes at night, and even 7 a.m. classes before work that nobody else attended. I changed into my clothes for work in the parking lot. There were even classes during the lunch hour. When you're nineteen or twenty years old and supporting yourself, you do what you have to do to get by. I would stay up until 2 a.m., getting four or five hours of sleep a night if I was lucky. Insomnia has been my constant companion since childhood, so even if I wasn't working or studying, it was hard for me to sleep.

I went to college for a total of nine years. It sounds like a long time, but I worked full time, sometimes working two jobs to make ends meet. I didn't need my degree, since I started making a decent amount of money as a paralegal and office manager, but I continued because I was determined to finish. I wanted to separate myself from my mother and eliminate any possibility of becoming like her. I thought my degree would be enough to do that.

It's *my* life!

CHAPTER THIRTEEN
MURDER WAS THE CASE THEY GAVE HIM

"Hardships often prepare ordinary people for
an extraordinary destiny." —C.S. Lewis

WHEN MY FUTURE HUSBAND mentioned buying a law practice in a small Northern Michigan town, it seemed like just the change I needed. I had been living in the same place for over three years, the longest time I'd spent in any town, and I knew that I was ready for something different. For me, a change always meant a move, so it didn't take much convincing.

I had never visited this town. It was a sleepy Northern Michigan town on the water. I love the water. That was all I needed to hear.

When I gave two weeks notice at my job, where I was by now managing another law office, they were less than happy. They tried everything to convince me to stay, even offering to pay for me to go to law school if I would continue managing the office. But I couldn't be swayed. I don't think that even a large check would have kept me from leaving. It was time for a change. When you grow up as a nomad, staying in one place is hard. Fighting the restless feelings, impossible.

This move meant more than settling my restless feelings. It was also an exciting opportunity to see if Gerry and I could create a business, all on our own. That meant lots of long hours working. Frankly, I couldn't think of anything better. When you have pain that you haven't dealt with, that you don't want to deal with, the easiest thing to do is pour yourself into your work. Society accepts that, no one questions it.

And did I have the opportunity to work long hours. It was an exciting time, and I was looking forward to the challenge of opening a law practice and setting into place all the systems I thought were necessary to run the perfect firm.

We spent days and nights working. The practice we were hoping to purchase belonged to an older attorney who, after a car accident, was finding it difficult to keep up. It seemed like a perfect way for us to start our own practice, with a built-in clientele. On our first day, it became clear that the attorney was terribly behind on his filings. He had a large number of clients, but it appeared as if little work was actually being done.

Gerry and I worked every weekend from sunup to sundown. We thought that if we put in enough hours we could turn the practice around. At first it seemed to be working. I was able to get the office filing caught up and a little more organized, and between the two of us, we completed nearly fifty mediation briefs. All briefs needed to be done in order to start settling some of the pending personal injury claims, which would bring in money for the firm. Or so we thought.

After nearly six months of continuous work, we were afforded an opportunity to start looking more closely at the finances of the office. It was shocking. We hadn't been paid, and we soon realized that the attorney had several bank accounts he had failed to disclose to us. He was funneling money out of the business by cashing checks and depositing the money in these accounts without our knowledge. He took retainers from clients and then told us they refused to pay. He cashed settlement checks and lied about the outcome of cases, or the amount that was dispersed to clients. We even discovered that he was in a Chapter 13 bankruptcy, and had previously lost his license for fraud and submitting false information to the court.

We didn't have any money when we came to Northern Michigan. We were living off of credit cards, residing in hotels. There happened to be a housing shortage in the town when we moved. Unable to find housing, the news that we were being cheated was more than either of us could handle. We struggled for another two months to try to work things out with the attorney. But after our discovery of his pending bankruptcy, we realized that he never intended to sell us his practice. There was nothing to sell. The whole thing was a scam. I took a night job at the Blockbuster Video next to the office, determined to try and keep us afloat financially.

On my birthday in 1999 we agreed to part ways with the attorney and his corrupt practice. Only one client agreed to leave with us, and she was broke. It was a new challenge for us, but we both seemed to thrive in these types of impossible situations, we almost needed the drama. After about two months, we were completely out of available lines of credit, and had less than nothing. We had found a rental house, but with no savings left we were eating hot dogs and noodles every night.

We had no business, no clients, little experience, and no budget for advertising. Apparently the demand was not high for 28-year-old lawyers with no connections or reputation.

It was a simple decision. I would get another job or two until we could find that one big case that would see us through to the other side. I began working a crazy, hectic schedule, getting to the office at around 8:00 or 8:30 a.m. and working with Gerry until around 3:00 p.m. Then Gerry would drive me home in our only car, and I would take a nap until 6:00 p.m. He would drive me to my other job that started at 7:00 p.m. I worked a twelve-hour shift until 7:00 a.m., working admissions in the E.R. of a hospital. Then Gerry would drive me back to the office. This schedule continued for about three months until, finally, Gerry's opportunity came.

Gerry was asked to be on the local court-appointed list. The court-appointed list is an index of attorneys who help indigent criminal defendants. It was something he had tried to get on numerous times, but had been denied. Gerry is passionate about criminal defense, and wanted to help those in need. The pay wasn't great - one low flat rate per case - but it covered our rent and minimal expenses. I was able to quit the extra jobs and focus on the office.

Most court-appointed attorneys do the work as a way to give back to the community, but we were doing it just to survive. We took each case very seriously, deciding early on that we would treat each person assigned to us as though they had paid us thousands of dollars. Since we couldn't afford advertising, we figured that these clients were the best form of promotion we could get.

The first case Gerry was assigned was a Criminal Sexual Conduct case that was less than two weeks from trial.

This client had another attorney, but that attorney was retiring, so they assigned the case to us. We worked on that file no less than 18 hours per day. We poured ourselves into the reports, combing over every detail. We did this for each and every case that was given to us. The office was reimbursed around $500 to $600 for each case. Calculating the hours we spent, we were paid minimum wage. But we persevered, knowing that at some point we would get a big break, a high profile case, and that it would turn everything around for us.

I was happy working those hours. It was easy for me. I had learned long ago that if I poured myself into my work, I would never have to think about all the pain I was in emotionally. I never had to relive the feelings of my past, or deal with the pain of being lonely on the holidays. Although Gerry and the office couldn't relieve all the pain I felt, the distractions of work and clients made it easy to push through each day. Much like other addicts, there was a high that I received from working. It felt as though I'd finally found something I was good at, and I wanted to maintain it for as long as possible. Plus, I was with my future husband, and after so many years alone, it felt great to be needed. We had no one except each other in our new, small town. We kept busy with our clients and continued to push ourselves. This pace continued for several years. Then, in September of 2001, everything changed for us.

The attack on the World Trade Center had just occurred when the front page of our local newspaper carried a disturbing image of a car being pulled from a local lake. Nearby, they found a young woman who they believed had been murdered. This made big news in our small town. The police had a suspect, her former boyfriend, but he was still at large. The story faded into the background, and another attorney we knew was appointed to the file. So we marched on with our other work.

By this time, we had moved out of our rental and into a home that we had just built. It wasn't fancy, but for the first time in my life I felt stable and reasonably settled. We were making enough money at the practice that we could afford to live. We were paying our bills, our student loans, and even had a small rainy-day fund.

When the fall air turned into the cold Northern Michigan winter, I began to feel tired and worn out. I attributed it to the schedule we were keeping, and the lack of healthy foods we were eating. I reasoned it would pass. I was 25, yet I hadn't been to a regular doctor since my car accident, although I saw a gynecologist for check-ups.

One day, a call came in from the court. It sounded urgent, and I immediately passed it through to Gerry. I could hear him from the other room. "Yes, judge. Whatever you need. I'll look for the fax." I could only hear his voice, but I could sense the excitement. I was thinking: *"No matter how tired you feel, you are going to feel even more tired soon."*

As Gerry hung up the phone, I could see his smile from down the hall.

"You're not going to believe it. The judge just called and asked if I would substitute in on the Torch River drowning case."

"What? I thought that guy already had an attorney."

"Turns out the attorney is taking a position in another county and can't continue with the case," Gerry said.

"When is the next hearing?" I asked. The last time we were in this position the case was two weeks from trial. I knew this was the opportunity we had been waiting for.

"The preliminary examination was scheduled for today, but they adjourned it when the attorney said he couldn't continue," Gerry explained. "They rescheduled the preliminary exam for December 11, so we have about four weeks before the hearing."

"OK, that's manageable."

"Well, we're also going to take over all his other files, so get ready," Gerry said with a grin.

I knew it was going to be a lot of work, but I was excited. This was a huge opportunity, and I knew we could handle whatever they threw at us. Just then the fax began to ring, and file after file began coming over. Gerry and I stood there smiling at each other. For the first time we both felt like we were doing the right thing. With this business there are no steady paychecks. Work comes and goes, so you never turn it down.

Our long hours continued, and we worked hard to be ready for the preliminary examination. As it turned out, the exam was scheduled for my birthday. In the years to follow, it became a joke that whenever there was a big hearing, it would be on my birthday. This would hold true for the next ten years and counting. It's now referred to as the Curse of Conway, the defendant's last name.

When you are defending someone who has been accused of killing a girlfriend, tensions run high. We appeared in the courtroom on a blustery December day to conduct the hearing, and it was packed. The room was filled with witnesses, police officers, and the friends and family of the victim. Gerry and I looked at each other, put on our game faces, and moved quietly through the crowd.

We could hear people in the gallery saying things, some under their breath, but most directly and loudly towards us. We had a good working relationship with the prosecutor, and Gerry had built a relationship with the police officers. He was known as tough, but fair. For this they all respected him, knowing that he would never be underhanded. The prosecutor asked to have a private conference with the judge. It was clear that we would have to address the growing restlessness of the crowd if the hearing was to move forward.

It was decided that all witnesses would be sequestered, and that anyone remaining in the courtroom must remain silent or face contempt of court and removal. This decision from the judge seemed to quiet the crowd down. The examinations began, and continued for most of the day and into the early evening. Around 5:30 p.m., the prosecution finally rested and the judge ruled. The case was bound over to Circuit Court, the next higher court, progressing the case towards trial. As we began packing up, the courtroom deputy approached us. He thought it was best if he walked us to our vehicle, as the crowd was unsettled again and our safety was becoming a concern.

They were angry and confused that such a terrible event could happen in their community. The victim was a local 21-year-old girl with a good family and a sunny disposition. She was liked by everyone who met her, and was known for her reddish hair and freckles, a popular girl who made friends easily. According to court documents, as she reached her 20s, she began to change. She met a guy and started to get serious about him. He was older than her, and hung out with the bad boys. He knew how to party and introduced her to that scene, eventually they both became hooked on cocaine. That's when she became someone that her friends and family no longer recognized.

She lost considerable weight, and only hung out with her boyfriend and his friends. Their relationship was on again, off again, but she wouldn't listen to warnings from her friends that the boyfriend wasn't such a nice guy. On the days before her death, she tried to leave him, and even ended up dating another guy. This struggle for independence and her ever-increasing addiction to cocaine fueled his rage. Court documents state he took her to a secluded place near the Torch River. They talked, and eventually he slammed her head into the steering wheel, knocking her unconscious. He then tried to make it appear she had an accident, putting her car into gear and pushing it into Torch Lake. The only problem was low water levels meant that the car never fully submerged. In fact, the water never got deeper than the bottom of the windows. He must have gone out into the water and held her under, killing her.

It had been a long day, and I was exhausted again. It had now been a month since my extreme fatigue had begun. We had a long drive back home, and I still had an exam to take. Since I hadn't finished my college degree, I was taking long distance learning classes, and

I could only enroll in one to two classes at a time. It was taking longer than I wanted, but I was determined to complete my degree no matter what. My exam had been scheduled for earlier in the day, but I had made arrangements with my professor to meet him at his home that evening, where he would proctor the test. So there I was, with a 45-minute drive back into town after an exhausting day, to take an exam. Gerry, exhausted, slept in the car. Luckily, I passed.

The office was busy and getting busier, so I wasn't surprised when I got a call from Gerry one afternoon while he was waiting in court. "Shen, I just talked to this local attorney, and he's thinking about joining the firm." He sounded excited. I was 26, Gerry only 31. We had big plans. Gerry and I had spent countless hours talking about how we wanted to grow our practice into the biggest and best firm in the area. This, we thought, was the first step toward achieving that dream.

"He's going to come over after lunch and take a look around the place." Since getting on the court appointed-list, our practice had continued to grow in other ways. We were doing divorce, custody, bankruptcy, estate planning, business and corporate law for small companies around town. Gerry and I were beginning to drown in the workload. I was excited that we might have a competent and experienced attorney to take on some of the work.

It all happened quickly, the attorney started two weeks later. He was older than Gerry by 17 years, had been a prosecuting attorney, and appeared to have all the answers. We thought it would be a good and natural fit. We agreed he would start on January 1, 2002. No buy in, just a handshake. Everything split 50/50. After all, as he put it, "My name is my buy in!"

Shortly after he started, my alarm bells and whistles were going off. But, as I had done so many times in the past, I thought I could fix it if I just worked harder. Our new partner soon started leaving early, missed court appearances, and even refused to give us his private cell phone number. He wouldn't take or return calls, pawned his work off on Gerry, me or the other staff, made inappropriate comments. The list goes on.

To add to the stress, it was becoming a real struggle for me to get out of bed each morning. Toward the end of January, Gerry was getting concerned. He had been trying to get me to the doctor for nearly a month. I had an appointment with my gynecologist at the end of the month. I reasoned that maybe it was hormonal. Perhaps my thyroid?

I had had issues ever since I'd gotten my first period. Often I would go several months without a period. It wasn't uncommon for me to miss three, four, or even five in a row. As I got older, the problem seemed to worsen. I could go even longer. By the time I was 17 or 18, doctors had told me that I would never be able to conceive a child. I wasn't sexually active then and, the news hadn't bothered me. I thought I would be a terrible mom anyway, given the role model I'd had, and reasoned that it was probably for the best.

The day of my appointment was Gerry's birthday, during the lunch hour. I explained to the doctor how tired I had been. Getting up in the morning was excruciating, and by 7:30 or 8:00 p.m. I was ready for bed. I had lost about 15 or 20 pounds, even though I was eating all the time. It was taking a toll on me and on my relationships. I felt depressed, but I couldn't get myself to snap out of it.

My doctor patiently listened to me, and said he thought it sounded like I was having thyroid issues. It was possible given my history, and it seemed a reasonable theory to me. He had me lie on the table and started my exam. Moments into the exam, I caught him with a puzzled look on his face. He paused, left the room, and came back moments later with a nurse. He looked at her, mumbling something I couldn't hear. I started to panic. I could feel that something was wrong. "Shen, just sit tight. I'll be right back," he said. *Everything is OK*, I thought.

I was lying on that table for what felt like an eternity. I was thinking about all the terrible things that could be wrong with me. Tumors. Cancer. *Just tell me, do I have months or days to live?* I was convinced that the doctor was going to give me a death sentence when he returned. Finally, he came back into the room, this time with something in hand. He began rubbing the device over my stomach. "Do you hear that?" he asked.

"Yes, my heart is beating pretty fast," I said. The whole time I was thinking: "*Of course it is, I'm dying.*"

"That's not your heartbeat," he said. I heard him, but I couldn't process it.

"What? What do you mean?" I asked.

"Shen, you're pregnant!"

Impossible. This is completely impossible.

"Are you sure? I thought I couldn't get pregnant."

"I'm sure!" he said. "You need to go to the hospital for an ultrasound so we can see how far along you are." He gave me instructions, only some of which I heard. I was in utter shock.

What was I going to tell Gerry?

How was I going to do this?

I couldn't be a mom. I had no idea how to raise a child. I had no one to ask. I hadn't even had a decent example of what a mom was. My mind started racing.

"Shen, can you hear me?" the doctor was asking me. "You need to get to the hospital right away."

"How far along am I?" I asked.

"I don't know, that's why you have to get the ultrasound. Given your previous symptoms, I would guess about 10 weeks," he suggested calmly, with a look on his face that suggested these kinds of things happened all the time.

After getting dressed, I dug through my purse, looking for my cell phone. I had to call Gerry, but what was I going to say? I made the call.

"How did it go?" he asked calmly. "Are you dying?" he joked.

I was quiet for a moment, and then said, "You're not going to believe this, but you have to meet me at the hospital!"

"What? Are you OK? What's going on?" I could hear his tone change quickly to real concern.

"I'm OK, but you're not going to believe it," I repeated.

"What's happening? Why do I have to come to the hosp —?"

I stopped him. "I'm pregnant."

"What? How is that possible?" He started asking questions quicker than I could answer. "I'll be right there." For the next few minutes I tried to compose myself, driving the two blocks to the hospital in a complete daze. As I sat in the waiting room, I wondered, *"What the hell am I going to do?"*

Just then, Gerry arrived, smiling. "Can you believe it!" he said, overjoyed.

I was shocked. Why was he so happy? *Didn't he remember all the stories about my childhood? Didn't he remember how crazy my mother was?*

"This is great. I can't wait to hear what they have to say," he continued. "I hope it's a girl. She'll probably be born in August." I was silent.

A nurse appeared. They mispronounced my name, a common occurrence for me.

As I was talking to the technician who was conducting the test, I could feel her skepticism. "How could you not know you were pregnant?" she asked.

I retold my story, a story that I would tell more than a thousand times. "OK, well, let's have a look." She started the ultrasound, and began taking all sorts of measurements. She was talking, but I wasn't listening. I could tell she was making calculations, and then I heard her say something definite. "May...middle to end of May, is when you are due!"

Are you kidding me? I was 26 years old, running a law practice in which I worked 50 plus hours a week, and was raised as a nomadic child with no sense of belonging. How was I going to have and raise a child and that was due to arrive in just four months?

I had been telling myself for nearly ten years that I would never have children. I was actually fine with it, and my husband was OK with it as well, though we talked about possibly adopting when things stabilized with the law practice. Now, I was flooded by memories from my childhood. I was living in utter fear.

It seemed like a terrible idea for me to be a mother. I didn't have the skills, the compassion, or the strength. I couldn't even take care of myself. I wasn't sleeping, suffering from insomnia more nights than not, and my diet was disgusting. I ate the cheapest and quickest foods I could find, not caring about what they were doing to my body. I felt I had no practical talents, and none of the qualities to make anyone believe that I was ready for this.

All the voices from my past were screaming in my head at once: "You will be just like your mother!" It was a feeling that was hard to shake, and suddenly it felt like it was becoming a reality. What if I was just like my mother? I had worked so hard to do everything in my power not to turn out like her, but in an instant it seemed completely out of my control. I had no role models for parenting, no guidance, and no parents to give me advice. How would I even know what to do?

Fear quickly turned to panic. I confided in Gerry. He tried to reassure me that I would do things very differently than my mother, that I could see how she had made mistakes and would make different choices. I would calm momentarily. But in the silence of the night, lying in bed staring at the ceiling, the fear would creep back in. What if I couldn't make different choices, what if the abuse had been ingrained into my genetic code? What if the pressure was too much for me?

In all the self-help books that I had started reading, all about overcoming the past and learning to move forward, everything repeated one common thread: The apple doesn't fall too far from the tree. All of my life, people warned me that I needed to be careful, because if my mom really was sick, then chances were I would be sick as well. They reasoned that, because she was an addict, there was a high probability that I would also have addiction issues. I wasn't sure that I disagreed.

While the psychologist in college had reassured me that I wasn't mentally ill, and even though I was a 26-year-old woman who didn't drink or smoke, I couldn't help but feel worried. Doubt controlled my every thought. I had been able to ward off the demons thus far, had proved the critics wrong, but still I was terrified that parenting was the one thing I should never attempt.

I was brought to tears a number of times by that very thought. Even today, I have days and moments when I question myself. But Gerry is good at reminding me that I am my own person, and that nobody can define me by the actions of my mother. It's a constant reminder that I need, and one that I think we all need. We make our own choices, good and bad. We control our own direction, our own lives and ourselves.

For me, the good news was that because I had found out so late this would be the shortest pregnancy in history. I wasn't given much time to sit and worry, which was probably for the best. By the time I found out, I was already five months pregnant, and closing in on a 10-day murder trial as Gerry's only assistant.

Gerry and I had talked about marriage several times. It was something we wanted to do, but the cost of a wedding was impossible for us. We were barely paying our bills, and had no idea how we could come up with the money. Traditionally it's the bride's parents who pay, but clearly I wouldn't be getting any help from my family. Gerry's family was quite large. By this time we had attended numerous family weddings together, and they were always huge affairs. There was no way I could afford such an extravagance.

Gerry and I postponed our marriage several times. We'd thought about doing a very small civil service in September of 2001, but then we were invited to a friend's wedding in Pennsylvania, and just couldn't seem to make it work out. Then September 11 occurred, followed closely by Gerry's parents announcing their decision to get divorced. It seemed that cancer had made his mother realize that life is too short to be unhappy. So, after years of arguments, talk of affairs and threats of divorce, they finally split their marriage. Their case raged on, with each parent vying for their children to side with them.

Now that we were pregnant, we could not wait for the perfect time anymore. We were married two weeks after we learned our baby was coming. We had less than ten people in attendance, some of whom are now in prison, then had a nice dinner out. Our friend, who was a judge, married us. It is perhaps my biggest life regret that we didn't have a proper white wedding with a big reception. Maybe we'll have a really rocking 25th anniversary instead.

CHAPTER FOURTEEN
BIRTH & BREAKDOWN

*"Everything in your life is a reflection of a choice you
have made. If you want a different result
make a different choice." —Unknown*

THE FIRST TIME I SAT IN A JAIL holding cell was when we went
to meet the defendant of the Moran Murder. I had interviewed plenty
of defendants for my role in the law office, but nothing really surprised me until I met William Conway. He was dressed in the black
and white striped Antrim County Jail shirt and pants that were issued
to all inmates. As the door closed behind him, we realized that we
were alone in the small holding cell with a man accused of a brutal
murder. There was no glass between us, no guard in the room to protect us. It was him and us.

He had blond hair, almost white, and it was meticulously groomed.
We never saw him with a hair out of place. Most striking, though,
were his pale blue, emotionless eyes.

The defendant was obsessed with his physical appearance.
He demanded that he have access to daily showers and additional
grooming supplies that were not available to other inmates. He was
tall, at least 6'1", and prided himself on his physique, which he had
honed as a former wrestler. He had a nervous grin, with large white
teeth that made me uneasy when he forced a smile. He was the type
of person who was vacant of emotion, perhaps he could be diagnosed
as a sociopath. His childhood had been terrible, at a young age his
father molested him and his brothers. There were also allegations
that his father would lead him and his two brothers out to seasonal

houses and cabins around the Torch Lake Area to break in and steal what they could, sometimes burning down the dwellings to cover up the crime. His brothers had served prison time for abuse of women and rape.

He was the type of guy that liked to be in control, so it was no surprise when our investigation revealed that he was a part-time deejay and drug-dealing hustler who could also set clients up with a female companion, for a fee. As part of one of his hustles, he would introduce a client to a female companion, provide party favors and, just when things got interesting, barge in and beat the person senseless, robbing him after.

Perhaps it was his past or the drugs, but although he answered all of our questions and participated in the conversation, deep within I had the feeling that he wasn't really there. This perception persisted over the next several times we met with him, but I couldn't put my finger on why until the trial. I was struck by how similar he seemed to all the men my mom had dated. I felt sorry for him, in a way I don't think anyone else could or would. I know that he killed someone, but still there was a sadness to him, a pain that he was covering with this macho attitude. He seemed very familiar to the men I'd known growing up.

In the weeks and months leading up to the trial, I spent a lot of time trying to train a new receptionist. I knew I was going to be out of the office for at least ten days during the trial, and was expecting to have the baby in early May. By this point, the doctors had determined that I was having complications, with low amniotic fluids and slow growth. They were hoping to induce labor as soon as possible, probably one or two months earlier than my due date.

The law partner who had talked such a big game wasn't helping. Clearly he was a disaster, but Gerry and I had so many other things going on that we put off dealing with him. Confrontation was never either of our strong suits, avoidance fits us better.

One Friday afternoon, Gerry asked our partner if he could assist with research for the murder case, to which he replied, "Nope, got plans already." This was a typical response. He was not a team player.

By the time trial rolled around, my belly was fully showing. In fact, I was beginning to have pregnancy dreams about the baby. Combined with my own fear of being the worst mother ever, I was dreaming about giving birth to the very girl that our client was accused of brutally killing. Every night I would wake up in a cold sweat, unable to lull myself back to sleep.

When the trial started, 45 minutes from our local hospital, the challenge really began. The doctor had put me on bed rest about two weeks before trial. I knew, even when he told me, that I could not stay on bed rest. There was no way. This case was too big and there was too much to do. Plus, we would only be paid at the conclusion of the case. So every other day, I would drive to the courthouse, sit through the morning session, drive to the hospital over lunch for a check up, then head back to the courthouse for the afternoon session. On one of the trips in, my doctor asked me how the bed rest was going.

"Oh, I'm really bored, but it's going okay," I said, in what I hoped was a convincing manner.

"Really?" he said. "It's funny, I saw you on the local news last night!"

Caught!

The circuit court judge in charge of the case warned me not to sit too close to the defendant during trial. They even put leg braces under his street clothes to ensure that he couldn't run. Tensions and emotions ran high as witness after witness was questioned. During the trial the prosecutor theorized that, after dyeing his hair black and attaching costume muttonchops and Elvis sunglasses, our client somehow broke into the victim's car and waited in the trunk, only to overtake her while she was driving.

We never bought into the idea of a surprise attack, and believed that the victim had asked to meet our client, probably because of a false promise of an apology or an offer of cocaine. We also never bought into their theory that he did this alone. He was a creature of habit, and never went anywhere without his lackeys. The case was a mess. At the conclusion of proofs, Gerry insisted those points while he was alone with the judge. The judge congratulated him on a job well done, saying "For his sake he hoped that he hadn't done too good of a job."

Several days later our client was convicted of open premeditated murder, and sentenced to life without parole. Whenever asked about the case, Gerry always says, "Justice was served." This is probably because, during our first meeting with the defendant, Gerry had asked him directly: "Did you do it?" The unflinching response: "Yeah, I did it. And it's your job to get me out of it!" We never asked the question again. It was easier not knowing the answer.

Two weeks later, I was at the hospital for my scheduled induction. I was nervous and anxious. In the short time I'd had to prepare myself mentally for giving birth, I had tried to avoid thoughts about the actual birth itself. But there I was at the hospital, at 5:00 a.m., being hooked up to various machines that would monitor the baby and me.

It was a long and tiring day. I became overwhelmingly concerned that I had done something to cause the baby harm by all my stress and running around. Suddenly I was terrified. The day seemed to drag on forever. Occasionally, the alarms on the machines would go off. Nurses would casually walk in, press the buttons, check on me, and leave. The pain would come and go in waves, until finally at around 9:30 p.m. the doctors decided it was time for me to push. Anxiety filled me, and cold tears ran down my face.

The room was filled with anxiety, as the doctors wanted this baby out quickly. The baby's heart rate was erratic and falling fast. I saw a glimpse of a scalpel, and realized that the doctor was about to perform an episiotomy. I begged not to be cut.

"No choice, we have to get the baby out," somebody said. I wasn't even sure who was speaking. At 10:12 p.m. the baby was out and they laid her on my chest. Tears were streaming down my face. I could see the smile on Gerry's face as he cut the umbilical cord. Before I could even grasp what had happened, they took the baby from me, cleaned her and wrapped her in blankets.

"Do you want to hold your baby for the last time?" I heard.

My mind began racing. *"What? Is my baby OK? What is going on?"* I couldn't contain myself. Doctors, nurses, Gerry, everyone was frantically running around the room. Before I could answer, the baby was being wheeled out.

The room quickly emptied. I was left by myself for what felt like an eternity. *"What happened, where is the baby? Did I take too many risks?"* Shortly a nurse returned. She could see that I was visibly upset and asked, "What's wrong?"

Choking back tears, I said, "Where is my baby, what is going on?"

"They had to take the baby to NICU, didn't they explain that to you?" she asked calmly. My baby was in the neonatal intensive care unit.

"No. All I heard was 'Do you want to hold your baby for the last time?' and then everyone left," I told her.

"Oh!" she said, concerned. "The baby is going to be fine, though they're worried about her breathing. Everyone is with her in the NICU. Here, let me help you clean up, and I will get you over there."

Sudden and complete relief. All of the anxiety about the type of mother I would be was completely gone in that moment. My only concern was for the health of my new baby girl. Later, when I was alone with our daughter in the NICU, I realized that I had two choices: (1) Give up and react the way everyone in my life expected, or (2) Do what I always had done: Make them scratch their heads and ask, "How does she do it?"

While alone with our daughter in the hospital, I had to make the choice. I chose the latter, and I continue to choose it each and every day. In fact, through the death of an innocent girl I had never met and the birth of my daughter, I had my own rebirth. I saw the sadness in the eyes of the murdered girl's parents. Her death, and the trial surrounding it, and the birth of my own daughter, showed me that life goes on no matter what. One person's life is cut short by a senseless act, but everyone else, the defendant, the victim's family, the attorneys, the staff, the jury is never the same again.

I was able to forgive myself, forgive the past, and begin working on creating a future that would not have been possible otherwise.

CHAPTER FIFTEEN
WHERE THERE'S SMOKE, THERE'S FIRE?

*"Life is what happens to you, while
you're busy making other plans."*
—Allen Saunders & John Lennon

ONE DAY AT A TIME. Day after day, I thought, *One day at a time.*
This was the strategy I employed with my daughter Sophia. As a
baby she was tiny, and I was amazed and overwhelmed at having
had so little time to prepare for her arrival. Car seat, crib, changing
table, diapers, onesies, and baby clothes, all were bought in a rush.
Add sleep deprivation to the mix, and the days became a fog. Sophia
wasn't a good sleeper. She slept in 20-minute intervals, and the
slightest noise woke her. It was helpful that I had learned to function on little sleep, because I wasn't getting very much with her. Her
infancy became a blur.

I focused on work, as I had for the previous seven years, caught
up in the need to keep making money. There were more days than I
would like to remember of bringing baby Sophia to the office with
me. I also learned how to get work done from home in those first
days. There is no maternity leave when you own your own business,
no help from family when you have none.

Getting back to work and functioning as a successful provider
was the priority for me as a mother. Being the working mom seemed
noble to me, and gave me fewer chances to ruin my precious baby
girl. The smaller the role I had in her upbringing, I rationalized, the
better chance she had.

I'd been pushing myself so long and so hard to work, work, work and make money, that I was convinced I had to be at work by 8:00 a.m. daily, and that I couldn't leave a moment before 5 p.m. every night. Gerry felt the same. We thought that by spending the time we did at work, we could provide Sophia with the nice things in life that neither of us had. In order to have it all, we needed to work harder, better, faster. We arranged for the best child care we could afford for Sophia, and enjoyed our precious few hours with her in the mornings and at night. We started with a nanny, who finally got her to sleep through the night, and then put her in a private Montessori school when she was 14 months.

Sophia's wisdom and powers of observation were clear from an early age. One day, as the three of us were driving on a cold autumn morning, we came upon an overlook where we could see the entire town. The trees blazed orange, red and yellow, and Grand Traverse Bay sparkled in the morning sun. We saw a stream of white smoke billowing towards the sky in the distance. Gerry turned to Sophia, perhaps four at the time. "Sophia, you know what they say? Where there's smoke there's fire."

Sophia, not missing a beat, retorted, "Do you see fire, daddy?"

"No?" Gerry said, wondering what was coming next.

"Then there's only smoke."

Gerry and I glanced at each other in profound amazement. Her childlike innocence had taught us both a valuable lesson. We should never assume anything. Just because something appears a certain way doesn't mean that it is that way. Sophia's assessment of that morning's scene became a catalyst for the reasons I needed to change. I wanted to change.

My mother had alcohol, drugs and men as her addiction. I had work and money as mine. Different, but both could cause the same destruction. I realized that Gerry and I could keep going on the treadmill forever. All work no play, and Sophia would soon no longer be a child. We both knew it. We often talk about the fact that if I hadn't gotten pregnant in the way I did, we would never have stopped. It was the reason we never had more children.

I had to step off the treadmill. For our daughter, for our family, for my sanity.

When I picked Sophia up from after-care, usually later then I was supposed to, she would climb into the back seat of the car, chatting and telling me about her day. I thought, *"This is ridiculous, there must be a better way."*

I felt like I hardly saw my little girl. I was consumed with the idea she and I were missing out on having a true mother/daughter relationship. I didn't want her going to any more summer schools, day camps, or after-care. I needed to change the way I worked. I realized I had real issues about the need to control things at work. Nobody was ever going to do it the right way. I was so sure that doing things my way was better. I needed to stop obsessing about everything, even how the office was being run. My new mantra became: If it doesn't get done, there is always tomorrow.

Slowly I began changing my schedule. First, I eliminated care before work. Then, after a few months, I began to pick her up after school and eliminated after-care. Soon, I was covering snow days and no-school days. Before I realized it, we got through a whole summer without putting her into a day camp. And, to my surprise, the work was still getting done. I had a real relationship forming with my daughter.

Sophia progressed from being a baby to a toddler, an elementary school student, and now a teenager. After she was born, I remember thinking, *"I'll be fine raising her until she's 12."* The age of 12 was the pivotal point when I decided that I could no longer tolerate how my mother was treating me and took action to get a better life. I was afraid Sophia would feel the same way, and want her independence from me. But she turned twelve, and then thirteen, and with each passing year I still breathe a sigh of relief. I don't know if I can let go totally of the feelings I had at that age about my mother, but I do know it's getting easier.

My special time with Sophia is after school, before Gerry comes home. I wouldn't give it up for the world. I grew into the role of the mom who has time to go to the bookstore or the library, and can help with school projects and make dinners. We have TV shows that we like to watch together, play games that I used to play with my grandmother, and have a lot of fun. I'd rather be around Sophia and my husband than anybody else I know. They have become my longest-lasting relationships and friends in life.

Another decision I made a long time ago was that, since I was brought up in a house of deceit, secrets, and lies, I would be completely honest with my own daughter, no matter what, when she asked questions. When I was a kid, I was often told that it was time to pack up all my stuff, but no one ever explained why. Maybe it was because my mom hadn't paid the rent, or a drug dealer was after her, or perhaps she was just bored with where she was. I never knew. I was not trusted with the truth. I wasn't even trusted with the truth about who my real father was. I thought I wasn't trusted because I had done something wrong. It was isolating and terrifying.

Honesty for me means that when Sophia has a question, I present her with the facts and let her come to her own conclusions. I want my daughter to understand the way the world works, in a way I'm not sure I ever did as a child. I want her to know that some people can be trusted, and others cannot. Most importantly, I want her to know that I trust her with information, and that no matter what, I will always love and support her first, before anything else. I want her to know that, no matter what decisions or choices she makes, she will never have to seek my approval.

I want her to be independent enough to make choices and decisions because she wants to, not because she thinks she needs to in order to keep me or Gerry or anyone else happy.

Sophia is not like most teens. She's worldly, wise, thoughtful and introspective. An old soul. I sometimes wonder if she is the keeper of my grandmother's spirit. She has a good sense of who she is, and has a great entrepreneurial spirit, even running her own design company and selling her work at a local store. She is her toughest critic. But watching her makes me want to be a better person. She has never been afraid to stand up for what she feels is right, a quality that I envy. She also has the wanderlust spirit that both my mom and grand-mother had. But with her, it seems that the travel is tied to wanting to see and understand different cultures, different landscapes, and different people. She wanders to find herself.

I want my daughter to have the best possible experiences growing up, but I also understand that even with the niceties in life, growing up isn't easy. We make it a point to travel to interesting places and experience life. We went to London and Paris when she was 11, her dream at the time; none of us wanted to come back. Perhaps we've all caught the wanderlust bug. Recently, we did a road trip all over the Southeast, from Michigan down through the Shenandoah National Park, all the way to Key West. Then we headed to New Orleans and rounded back home. The point of these trips is to experience new culture, new food, and new people. We want to expand and grow as a family, and appreciate the time we have together.

Sophia knows about my experience in foster care and my difficult beginnings. This knowledge came when she first asked where my mother was, and whether or not she was still alive. I told her the truth. When I asked her recently what she thought about the way I grew up, she paused momentarily, and then said, "It seems like their loss." She continued, "I mean, they clearly didn't want to be parents, and now they've missed out on knowing you." It was a simple and compelling statement to me. One of my biggest fears in becoming a parent was that I would treat my daughter in the same way my parents treated me. But, in listening to Sophia describe it, I realized that we each make our own mistakes. Everything is a choice. I have to own mine, and everyone else gets to own theirs.

I enjoy the freedom that owning our own business provides. I was able to let go of my fear once I realized that the sun continues to rise and fall and that, regardless of what each new day brings, we still have a roof over our heads. When you release the fear, you can allow yourself to forgive a little easier, and you can allow for the time and space needed to create your own life, your own story on your own terms.

For the first time ever, my story feels like it's truly becoming my own.

CHAPTER SIXTEEN
FROM FOSTER CARE TO KING OF SCOTS

"Insanity doesn't run in my family. Rather it strolls through taking its time, getting to know everyone personally." —Unknown

I HAVE ALWAYS BEEN INTERESTED in genealogy, and during that summer with my dad I told him about the work I had done to trace my family. That included name research, heritage information, database and immigration records, etc. But I had come up empty for the most part. Several days later, my father produced a softbound blue book and gave it to me. It was his mother's family history, dating back to the early 1600s, and chronicled their trip along the Oregon Trail to the Pacific Northwest in the 1800s. I have read that book no less than ten times over the course of my life. When I first received it, it felt like a high privilege. I had been lied to so many times about my father that being able to connect with the names, birth dates and facts of these people seemed like a fairy tale.

From my time in the hospital after my car accident, when it felt like I was completely alone in the world, to receiving this book, I had lived in a haze, with no clear idea of who I was. Suddenly I realized I might be able to determine where I fit into the world. However, being able to trace your family back to the tenth century can be overwhelming.

This bound book became a cherished possession. Carefully turning the discolored pages, the original book was published in the mid 1970s, before I was born, I somehow felt closer to family than I had ever felt before. Seeing all of these names, stories, dates and information began to stoke the fire, compelling me to learn more about who I was and where I came from.

When I first started my research, before ancestry records were online, I had to make a lot of inter-library requests, and thumb through pages and volumes of useless information, trying to find that one break I was looking for. I spent lots of time writing and mailing letters to various court clerks, register of deeds and vital records offices, trying to locate any missing piece to the puzzle. After a while, the process itself became cathartic.

I kept my father's book safe for many years, not really sure what I could do with the information. As technology changed around the time my daughter was born, I decided to start a family tree on ancestry. com. I got the urge to put all the information from the book onto the website, so that Sophia would have it if she ever grew curious about her family origins. I started with her, and began working all sides of the family, my husband's and my own.

It became a new addiction. I spent countless hours clicking on documents, searching the web, verifying ideas, memories, and various other pieces I could find.

I initially started with my father's mother's side, because I had so much information. That data soon led to several interesting connections on my father's father's side as well. Soon, I had found several relatives who fought in the American Revolution. In fact, I had found relatives that fought in every American war. I kept going. I'm still going. Every day I find new pieces, new information, and it's still a complete thrill.

Some of these revelations led me to join groups and organizations, like the Daughters of the American Revolution, where I was able to rejoice in and celebrate discoveries with others. The members also seemed to be trying to patch the pieces of their relatives' lives together, in order to heal themselves in some way. This is not true for everyone, of course, but those who are drawn to genealogy always seem to find some extra meaning in unearthing a missing piece of their history. I think this is especially true for those who don't have close ties with immediate family members.

I've also started working on my mother's family, which has proven more challenging. I'm still struggling to find her father, and any information about her mother's marriages. I am hopeful those answers might shed light on the struggles my mother experienced, and help me to close some of the wounds on that side of my family.

I have traced parts of the direct family line back to the year 839, and I'm still going. It's not just about finding my link to these amazing people, although knowing that I am part of such a long and traceable line makes me feel far more connected than I ever could have imagined. I went from being a throwaway child, left to age out of the foster care system, told again and again that I was worthless and not worth loving, to finding out that my ancestors were royalty, inventors, people of persuasion and influence. I discovered a great-grandmother who was the only literate person in a royal court, and who advised her husband the king on legislative orders. It makes me proud, and I hope Sophia will enjoy discovering her heritage when she starts having a family of her own. I want her to see the connections that have led her to this life, some one thousand years later.

PART TWO: FIGURING OUT "NORMAL"

CHAPTER SEVENTEEN
RELATIONSHIPS AREN'T AUTOMATIC

"The worst thing about being lied to is knowing
you weren't worth the truth." — Unknown

ABOUT 1.6 MILLION PEOPLE are in prison in the United States. Of those, it is estimated that approximately 1.3 million have been foster kids at some point in their lives. Learning these facts changed how I saw my own story.

How did I make it when all these other people did not? How did I beat the odds? I know that, from a very young age, I thought about escaping. The only way I ever saw people get out of the areas we lived in was through work, and getting a better job meant going to college. I'm not smarter than anyone else. I'm clearly not luckier. But, without even knowing, I made a decision to be different than my mother. I set my sights on that goal, moving forward no matter the result. Regardless of the obstacle, I found a way to survive. I was not going to allow anything to break me. It was me against the world. *I'll show them what a success I can be by not following in her footsteps.* For me, rebellion was doing everything I could possibly do to keep from becoming like my mother.

I'm not like my mother. I could never be so irresponsible and selfish, especially to my own daughter. Being a mom was the fuel for my desire to be a better person. Now that I understand who I am, I have the power to create whatever it is that I want. That doesn't mean I don't still face obstacles. Relationships are still difficult for me. I suspect that they always will be. But now I choose the relationships that fulfill me, and nurture my spirit. I only have room in my life for people that enrich me, and I refuse to create excuses for those that don't.

MY MOTHER

Today, my mother has become all but a faded memory. I have lived without her longer that I ever lived with her, and I haven't heard from her since I got the card in the hospital when I was seventeen. Thoughts and memories of her come to me less and less. I only think of her near her birthday, or when someone asks me about my parents. In the moments that I allow myself to dwell on the pain that she caused me in my childhood, I quickly remind myself that even as a child, I was in control of my own life. I made decisions, sometimes difficult and painful ones, which led me to where I am today. I have no anger, no hatred, and no ill will. I simply wish her, as I would any stranger, the best.

MY STEPFATHER

Prior to his recent death, my stepfather, who treated me terribly as a child, who lied, who abandoned me, would still pick up the phone and stand in as family from time to time. When I wanted someone from my family to attend my wedding, it was him I called. I had no one else. The sad thing is that, no matter how badly someone treats you, there's a comforting familiarity with the dysfunction. It is this undeniable fact that I think leads to most of the unsuccessful foster care placements. No matter how hard a foster family tries, they will never be the family of that child. My stepfather and I had shared experiences and memories, and we both expressed a hatred for my mother.

As a teen, I had become so angry and disgusted with my mother that my stepfather ended up looking like the good guy. That was partly because he hadn't completely disappeared from my life, partly because he actually managed to settle down. Over the years, I tried to put more of the blame on my mother. It was easy since she wasn't around, and everyone else was eager to allow her to accept the blame as well. But my stepfather was calculated and manipulative, qualities he never lost over all those years, though I tried to convince myself they didn't exist any longer so I could finally have family.

Near the end of his life, he remarried and moved to the Traverse City area, ostensibly to be near Sophia, Gerry and I. We had kept in touch over the years, talking weekly and seeing each other on holidays. We were excited at first to have family so close, and thrilled by the idea of local grandparents for Sophia. At the time, I was working on myself, working on forgiveness. It seemed like a good start to my healing, as other options were few.

As first, my stepfather and his wife needed a little help with the move while they got on their feet. We ended up paying their mortgage, and providing money for miscellaneous expenses for several months. They were lovely to us, and it was great to have them around. But I had some red flags. Sophia stayed with them occasionally for the day. When I picked her up she was always in her room, watching TV alone. This triggered all the memories I had of being locked in my room alone, of how isolated I'd felt, and I began to worry about Sophia spending time with them unsupervised.

Eventually we made it known that we could not continue to support them indefinitely. My stepdad had it good, and was not making any attempt to take over the payments or seek employment. He was outraged that I would do this to my only family, especially after all that he had done for me. Once the money from us was gone, so was he. Within two months they moved out of town without saying goodbye. It was the last I ever heard from him.

Perhaps it was the way they treated us when we no longer supported him, but in the process of trying to resolve my issues from the past, sorting through the lies, I decided that I needed to understand why my parents had moved so much when I was a child. I figured that, without the answers, I would never truly be able to move forward and forgive. My stepfather always told me that he'd been on the run from the law in his hometown of Brockton, Massachusetts since his late teens, before he had met my mother. In fact, when we visited his family there as a child, it was always under the cloak of secrecy. No one was ever allowed to know we were visiting, I guess because he thought he would be arrested on outstanding warrants. I thought that if I knew about his past, it might explain more about my own childhood.

I decided to contact a private investigator whom we frequently used through the course of our law practice. He was able to help track down a reputable private investigator in the Brockton area. I gave him the abbreviated story: I had grown up with a man that I thought was my father. During my childhood, he revealed that he had gotten into some trouble during his youth, and after a run in with the law, he was let out on bond, and ran. My question for the investigator was simple: "What was he running from?"

I shared with the investigator the limited information I had. That included his alias, his family's name, his date of birth and his social security number, or at least the ones he was using. The investigator told me he had a few connections in the county he could check with as it was a small town and even smaller courthouse. He said he would get back to me shortly.

As I was lying in bed that night, my mind wandered. *What was so bad that my father changed his identity and spent his entire life on the run from it?* Nobody else I knew seemed to be this fearful of his or her home, with the exception of my brother and me. Crazy scenarios kept running through my head over the next several weeks. Were people other than the police after him? Had he testified against someone?

The call came. "Shen, I have some good news and bad news," the voice said. I knew exactly who it was. The private investigator had the distinct sounds of a Boston accent mixed with a lifetime of cigarette smoking. You could almost smell his tobacco-soaked office waft through the phone lines.

"Let's have it," I said. I had prepared myself for any possibility. Murder, drugs, theft. I was determined to handle whatever the investigator threw my way.

"I spent several hours at the Brockton courthouse. I was able to find a few minor charges that Steve was involved in, mostly writing bad checks and a larceny by conversion, or theft. It does appear that he might have missed a court date, but the courthouse had a fire and all pertinent documents were lost." By the tone in his rough voice, I thought he might be joking.

"You're kidding, right? That's it?" I was waiting for the roughness of his voice to break out in a cackle. I didn't happen.

"I'm not kidding," he stated. "Your father is not wanted by any courts, so unless someone is looking for him, I'd say he's been running from a ghost. Frankly, given the amount of time that's passed, I figure even if he was in some trouble they've forgotten all about him by now."

My mind was racing. It was starting to feel like that call to my Uncle Jim all those years before.

I was stunned. I fell silent. "Hello?" the voice broke in.

"I'm still here," I said. "I just can't believe it. What about the feds?" I knew I was grasping. If the federal government was after him, they would have picked him up a lifetime ago, but I had to ask.

"There's nothing in the federal system about him," the detective answered. "He's not wanted!" I knew he was trying to convince me.

I'd spent my whole childhood running from absolutely nothing!

After we stopped talking, I would think of my stepfather occasionally, mostly on his birthday, or when the Red Sox won the World Series, or the Patriots won the Super Bowl. I hoped that he was happy.

Then, while working on this book, I received a phone call. I was at the office, and I could see the look of confusion on our secretary's face. "Shen, there is a gentleman on the phone who is saying your father passed away." I knew immediately that it must be my brother. "Al," I said as I picked up the phone. "If you're calling me, it can't be good news."

I was trying to make it light-hearted, but the truth was I hadn't heard from my brother in years. He had stayed in Muskegon, eventually marrying and having two children, both now fully grown. We have a strange relationship. We don't speak unless it's absolutely necessary. I think it's too painful for us to interact with each other, as we are reminded of the past. We are both different people now, in very different parts of our lives. I wished it wasn't this way, but you don't always get to choose the way a relationship with someone evolves.

"Steve died," my brother said, flatly. I could hear the pain in his voice. I don't know how my brother remained so close to my stepfather all those years, but somehow they were able to stay in touch in spite of the past. Perhaps my brother was still looking for his forever family as well.

"What happened?" I asked, wondering if his chronic illness had been responsible.

"I don't know," Al stated. "The police were just here, letting me know. I haven't even talked to his wife."

"How are you taking it?" I asked. I knew the answer. I could tell he was struggling, but I was stretching to keep the conversation going.

"I'm pretty upset, but I'll be okay."

"Do you know any of the details, when the funeral will be, or anything?" I wasn't completely sure why I was asking, but it seemed like the right thing to do.

"I don't know anything."

"Well, call me back when you hear something. I'm here." That's all I said. I couldn't think of anything else.

"Ok, I just wanted you to know. I'll call you later this week."

And that was that. My stepfather had died. Days passed into weeks, and I never heard from my brother again. Picking up the phone seemed impossible for me. I stumbled across my stepfather's obituary in an online search. It was difficult to read. It felt as though I was reading an obituary for a stranger. The man described was not the man I knew. But it was the way he would have wanted it, a generic story that mentioned nothing of who he really was. It didn't even use his real name, or mention my brother or me. It was all made up.

In the end, I suppose it doesn't matter. For me, the child that suffered at his hand, the adult who still can't gain understanding of the relationship, I am left only with a sense of peace. Perhaps the feelings I had when reading his obituary, where he felt like a stranger, hold true. Perhaps I never did know him, and now I never will.

MY FATHER

Deep down I long for a family connection. I think everyone does. I hadn't given up on trying to establish a rapport with my birth father, though our relationship suffered numerous ongoing setbacks. Gerry and I visited him for a few days in 2000. I wanted my future husband to get to know someone in my family and with the uncertainty of the law office, Gerry and I were looking for other options. But after our wedding and Sophia's birth, neither of which my father managed to attend, I gave up on him.

My father was still sending Christmas cards, but I just couldn't respond. I had almost no energy left to try and engage in a relationship with him. The cards felt so meaningless. *Too little, too late,* I thought with the arrival of each one. I was content to never see him again. This contentment was reinforced when, out of the blue, I received a card and letter from Carol, his wife. She went on for two pages about how I was a selfish person for ignoring my father's need to connect with me. This sent me into a rage. The audacity, I thought. Any chance of reconciling our relationship was completely off the table.

Finally, after three years of prompting, I started a Facebook account. I had been reluctant at first, because I thought that my mother might try to contact me, or even worse ask for money like my stepfather. I had only been on it a few months when a friend request from my dad popped up in my inbox. *This is exactly why I didn't want to get on.* I ignored it for a month. When Gerry asked me what I was afraid of, it was easy to respond. Disappointment. I was so tired of the disappointment.

Then I considered the possibilities. I knew I needed to confront the issues, I knew that I needed to find forgiveness. Perhaps this was my opportunity to lay it all on the line, like I had wanted to do so many years before during our first meeting.

I accepted the friend request, and sent him a very lengthy and brutally honest message listing all the ways in which I thought he was a disappointment. I explained why it was difficult for me to forget the past and act like a father and daughter. I was looking for one thing. An apology.

I didn't get it.

What I did get was a song-and-dance filled with excuses about his life, his difficulties, and reasons why he didn't fight to be with me. I had no patience for it. The anger was killing me, and I knew I had to release it. I just didn't know how. I thought I needed his apology to make myself forgive. Ultimately, as I was meditating in yoga class, a practice that I had taken up to help me cope with daily pressures, I became overwhelmed with a sense of peace. I realized that I may never get the apology in the style and manner that I expected, and that I had been choosing to stay bitter and angry. Just like that, I found forgiveness.

That Christmas, my father sent Sophia a gift. As she opened it, she asked when she was going to meet her grandfather. She was ten. I sent him a message, relating how thankful we were for the gift, and told him that Sophia wanted to meet him. He visited three weeks later, in the middle of a harsh Northern Michigan winter.

His wife Carol had passed away two years prior, so perhaps the timing was right for a new beginning to our relationship. It was the first time he had shown up since I graduated from high school. Gerry took him ice fishing, and they spent time together bonding. It took a lot of pressure off of me. I was nervous, and keeping him busy with activities was a way for me to cope. It was a short visit. After he left I realized I had finally started to do my work on our relationship, and that he had his own work to do in turn. At last, I had the beginnings of an honest and truthful connection with a real parent.

Then one day, after I taped a radio interview on my experience in the foster care system, I got this beautiful and unexpected e-mail from my father:

As I get older, I find myself questioning decisions and lack of decisions that I have made over my life. So with a heavy heart I do hereby apologize to my daughter. I apologize for not being the man I was supposed to be. I apologize for not being the protector from demons under your bed, imagined and real. I apologize for not being there at your school play, for not packing the love in your lunch box that you so needed. I apologize for not being able to pick you up when you fell, and give you the warmth of a hug, to dry your tears from a skinned knee. I apologize for not being there when you got to wear your first dress for that special night out. I apologize for not scaring off that first boyfriend of questionable intentions. I apologize for the lack of respect you have gotten for going through the first half of your life without a father. I apologize for missing your wedding, at a time when "I" needed to be by your side. I apologize for missing the birth of your beautiful daughter, a moment I can never regret more. I apologize for being selfish, because I thought chasing the almighty buck was more important than seeing the glory of family, love and togetherness. But more than anything, I apologize for not being man enough to throw out all the indecisions and come to your rescue when we both needed so much to cling on to and make our lives better. For all these things I APOLOGIZE. They say time heals all wounds, but time never heals a broken heart. Please forgive me!

As I write these apologies there are also things I won't apologize for. I won't apologize for bringing you into this world. For the day you were born when your eyes were full of won-

derment and awe. I won't apologize for the joy you gave me when you took your first steps. For the love I REALLY felt when I awoke with you in my arms only to find us both soaked with the surprise of a late diaper change. But more than all that, You have become the person the world needs more of. You have become a leader. As the great and powerful Oz said, "A Doer of Good Deeds." That person is trying to right the wrongs in the world, caused by people like me. You are the light at the end of the tunnel. And that my sweet daughter I will never apologize for. I will always love you... DAD

Finally the apology I had been looking for, for over twenty years.

MY IN-LAWS

When Gerry and I got together, and it was clear that we were going to stay together, I was excited that he had parents who were still married, two sisters and a very large extended family. At last, a normal family that I could bond with and share holidays.

My enthusiasm promptly faded when the reality of his family life became clear.

When Gerry and I met in September of 1997, we went on one date, and within a few weeks had moved in together. It just happened, there was no real discussion. Gerry had graduated from law school and was then studying for the bar exam, which was a full time job. He had been denied a bar loan[5] and had taken out student loans to pay for law school. When he started, his father was working for a local bank that provided the loans for Gerry. His father asked him how he wanted to handle the interest on the loans, and Gerry told his father that he wanted to defer the interest, because he could not afford to make payments while going to school. This didn't sit well with his father. He knew that deferring the hefty 13% interest would be more

---

5   A loan that helps keep you afloat when you are studying for the bar. It's similar to a student loan.

costly in the end. Instead, he offered to make the interest payments for him.

It turns out that the payments were never made. There have been varying stories on why or how this happened, but bottom line, the payments weren't made, ruining Gerry's credit. Of course, he didn't find out about this until he was denied a store card at a major retailer. Ultimately his credit became such an issue that it had to be explained when he applied for his license to practice law.

We lived together so he wouldn't have to pay rent. I sublet my apartment, because it was more expensive than his, and we moved in together. Gerry had a car when we first met, but it was in dire need of many repairs, repairs no one could afford, so I began driving him when he needed to go somewhere. My day would look something like this: I drove into work by this time working for a larger law firm, and during my lunch hour, I drove home to pick up Gerry, and brought him to the other side of town to his study group. Then I drove back to work. After work, I would drive to pick him up from study group and drop him off back to the apartment. Then, I would go to school to take more classes toward my own degree. I was working to pay our combined bills, while he put all of his efforts into studying for the bar exam.

It appeared from the outside that Gerry was not close to his family, he rarely talked about them. Our apartment was a small, run-down one bedroom, the only entrance was a rickety wooden staircase at the back of the soon-to-be condemned building. It was above a small retail store called The Rosary that sold rosaries and other religious paraphernalia. During the day the heat was unbearable, reaching scorching heights. At night, when the store closed, the owner turned off the heat to the entire building. It made for some long and blustery nights. But the view from the kitchen was spectacular. Through a small window, maybe twelve inches by fifteen inches, we could see the dome of the Lansing Capitol building, aglow at night.

One day, driving home to pick Gerry up for his study group, I pulled into our assigned parking space, maneuvering my car between the two storefronts and pulling my side mirrors in so as not to hit the buildings. Coming to a stop, I noticed some cars there that I hadn't seen before. I walked up the back stairs, opened the door and came in, finding Gerry with his mother and sister. It was the first time I'd met them.

I remember immediately becoming uneasy as I introduced myself. His mom was sitting in the corner chair, a chair Gerry had inherited from his deceased grandmother. I sat quietly on the couch. Gerry was teasing his mom about her wig, she was receiving chemotherapy at the time for breast cancer treatment. Gerry was already completely bald in his 20s, and soon the back-and-forth teasing began. Before I knew it, his mother had grabbed her wig and thrown it across the room. Everyone was laughing, so I joined in. The encounter was brief, within minutes his mom and sister left, but it stuck with me that she never shook my hand or even said "Hello."

Gerry explained that he and his mother had been close during his childhood, joining forces to survive the wrath of his father who had a terrible temper. But since his mother had been diagnosed with cancer, she seemed to be changing. She seemed bitter, and was very different than the nurturing fifth grade teacher he had described. Given these circumstances, I tried to roll her lack of interest in being cordial to me off my back.

Initially, I chalked up her frostiness to the stress surrounding her cancer treatments, but it soon became clear that Gerry's mom didn't approve of me, no matter what she was going through. Parents had always seemed to like me, so this was a first. Although I've never completely understood the source of her venom, I assumed that since I was a foster child, she considered me to be lower class. I didn't come from good enough stock.

On our first Christmas together, I pooled all the money I had and bought a trip to Las Vegas to celebrate Gerry's hard work on the bar exam. I've always felt a connection with Las Vegas because of the time I spent there as a child. It seemed the closest thing to a home for me, plus it made for a very inexpensive destination. After spending

Christmas alone for several years, I thought inventing a new holiday vacation tradition with Gerry would be fun. But Gerry's mom was furious that I'd booked it for the day after Christmas, as she'd been looking forward to spending time with him.

Years later, when we excitedly told Gerry's family the news: "We're pregnant!" I thought that it might finally bring the clan together. I had hoped, post-divorce, that Gerry's mom would be happier, and less focused on me. That hope quickly disappeared when she asked me, "Are you sure it's Gerry's?"

After about three years of running our own business, Gerry and I purchased a house on a lake. We thought it would be a great place to invite friends and family for summer visits, barbecues, boat rides and fishing. He said that he and his mom used to talk about buying a cottage up north when he was a kid, and spending the summers on a lake. The primary purpose of the house was to entertain; it's located on a magnificent lake, approximately 2,500 acres. The first time Gerry's mother, stepfather and sister came for a visit, I was excited but also very nervous. I knew that I wasn't their favorite person, but I thought that I had made improvements with Gerry's mom. She had lived with us for a few months after Sophia was born, and although she hadn't agreed with all of our parenting decisions, I thought she could see how hard we were both working. I confided in a friend about how nervous I was for the event. I shared countless examples of times I hadn't done things right in their eyes, and worried over how I could get his mother to really like me. Perhaps if I could get this visit to go smoothly, it would change everything.

I had begun to hone my cooking skills, learning as I went. It was going to be a long weekend, and I wanted to serve a great home-cooked meal for their first night. My friend very sweetly said that she would help me prepare this whole meal from scratch. I was eagerly looking forward to being the hostess-with-the-mostest.

After spending two full days in the kitchen preparing, and meticulously setting the dining room table to be sure that I hadn't missed a thing, I was ready to show off my work. After everyone had arrived and gone outside to enjoy and relax by the water, I called them in to dinner. My mother-in-law sat down at the table while I happily scanned the room, listening to the oohs and aahs of the other guests admiring the food and the beautifully decorated table. Then, almost as quickly as they sat down, my mother-in-law abruptly stood up and proclaimed, "What, there's no salad?" She then left the room, never to return.

I was in absolute shock. My dream of the happy extended family evaporated before my eyes.

Although Gerry doesn't get along with his family, he still feels immense guilt for not being around them more. They love him, but he doesn't want to visit them by himself because it's painful for him. If I go with him they won't accept me, and if I don't go it's not the right thing. Gerry's family believes that I'm cutting him off from them, that I've taken their son away. Yet, this guy was on the verge of being homeless and I gave him shelter, rent, food, transportation, inspiration, acted as a study partner, and most importantly loved him. It's always a very reflective time for me when Gerry talks about his family. I see the love he has for them, and the pain that he feels for not being around them. I also see the other side of his pain when they make comments about me, or disrespect me in some way. He is caught in a trap, and I wonder if maybe I am the lucky one, abandoned by my parents but no longer feeling the pain.

Because I spent much of my life being told how worthless I was, I will not accept having those kind of people in my life any longer, and refuse to expose my daughter to such negativity. I don't think anyone should be treated that way, and I certainly will not allow Sophia to think it's okay to endure such belittlement.

Gerry, Sophia and I love each other. We are not only family, but also friends. Perhaps we only need each other. Perhaps Sophia has it right after all: "Just look at how much fun we have, we don't need anything else." I believe she is absolutely right.

CHAPTER EIGHTEEN
YOU CAN'T ALWAYS RUN, YOU DON'T ALWAYS HAVE TO HIDE

"When I let go of what I am, I become what I might be." —Lao Tzu

I HAVE SPENT MY ENTIRE LIFE RUNNING. Originally, we were running from the police, landlords, or secrets that I still haven't begun to uncover. Perhaps we were running from phantoms, born of my stepfather and mother's paranoid minds. Although my parents were legally relieved of their parenting duties, my need to run still hasn't released its hold.

I was running from the pain of my past, from the truth of what I thought I was, what I thought I should be, and from myself. Running has always been easier than facing the facts, yet as I have aged, my ability and desire to run have faded. I've come to face the pain of my past. I am confronting it, the best I can, when I can.

The biggest lesson I have learned during my ultra-marathon is that the universe has a way of handling some of the confrontation for you.

Case in point: After Gerry and I mustered the courage to stand up to his former partner and air our concerns that the relationship wasn't working, we were served with a lawsuit from him the following day. He claimed that we had wronged him by leaving, and that he deserved to be paid. In a sense he was right. Without us to market, work the practice, clientele and cases, he had nothing.

That lawsuit almost financially, emotionally, and physically ruined us. We were both tested. Coping with a new daughter, a new marriage and a practice that was barely holding on was a major challenge. Our former partner waged a campaign of popular opinion. He told anyone who would listen how badly he was injured by our actions. He was a storyteller, and boy did he talk. For ten years our name was dragged through the mud. According to him, we were liars and cheats, Gerry would soon be disbarred, and a bankruptcy was impending. These were all reasons for fellow lawyers to distrust us, and for potential clients to steer clear of us.

We lasted, though. Through all the bad-mouthing, we held our heads high, and never returned the shots he took at us. Even though it was a struggle, the universe kept us safe in ways we didn't understand at the time.

Flash-forward another eleven years, and that same former partner found himself in a lawsuit with a former client. The client had been to prison and, after being released, won the lottery. He was now a multi-millionaire, with money to spend. It turns out that our old partner had entered into a business deal with his client, but as in our situation had brought no money to the table. Our former partner once again brought his name, connections and legal acumen, and then demanded to take half of everything.

After a drawn-out civil court proceeding, the client was victorious. As part of the case, the judge awarded an additional $350,000 to cover legal fees and sanctions. This was too much for our former partner to handle, so he attempted to hire an amateur hit man to end the life of the opposing counsel. In his mind, this would end the lawsuit, allowing business-as-usual to resume. Instead, the would-be hit man, fearing a set up, recorded their conversations. The details of the plan were undeniable. In the end the lawyer pled guilty to a charge that would see him serve hard time in prison.

I worry about my ability to attract these types of people into my life. While all I want is to be part of a family, or something bigger, I seem to attract creep after creep. The con-man, if you will. There must be a reason, one cannot simply have this much bad luck, after all. It's clear that it is me who is attracting these people, and it is me who can change that.

My father recently told me a story illustrating the type of mentality my parents had when I was born. They were living in California at the time, and Squeaky Fromme, a member of the Manson Gang, had recently tried to assassinate President Gerald Ford. My parents were with a group of friends in December, and mused that Charles Manson needed a Christmas card to cheer him up. They all thought this was a great idea, and popped one in the mailbox. Days later, the FBI swarmed the apartment, interviewing each one of them individually. They had put a return address on their card. Perhaps this was why I was not allowed into the FBI's training program.

What else can I say about my mom and dad? They thought it was a great idea to send a Christmas card to Charles Manson. They were constantly on drugs, not thinking of the consequences of their actions, and newborn me seemed to provide little incentive for them to clean up their acts and behave like grown-ups.

Slowly, I am concluding that forgiveness is mine and mine alone. It doesn't take two people. It only takes me to forgive myself and forgive the person who caused me to feel the way I did in the first place. In writing this book, several people kept asking me how it was going to end.

They too seemed to be looking for a fairy tale ending, the happy conclusion that I had given up on so many years before. "When are you going to track down your mother?" they would ask. It's then that I understand they haven't been able to grasp the totality of my story. Reconciliation isn't possible. The fairy tale ending isn't coming.

It is impossible for me to allow a woman back into my life who has caused such irreparable damage. A woman who has now become just the person who gave me life, content in not knowing whether I lived or died. In fact, when people ask about her, I am somehow transported back in time. Back to the courtroom. Back to wondering if she would show up to claim me. I am the same child, holding the same hurt.

I have no desire to find my mother. Perhaps it is because of the pain and disappointment I initially felt after finding my father. I believe that I would experience no satisfaction in a meeting with her. After numerous years of working through the pain of what happened to me, and growing emotionally as a result, I have come to accept that I cannot change the past or other people.

For years, I struggled to make people understand that I was really okay with the way things turned out. I didn't want to dredge up the past. I hold no ill will towards my mother, father, or stepfather. They made their decisions, and I made mine. None of us can take them back. When I began writing this book, I spent long hours asking myself the real reason I wanted to write it. Was I trying to cause pain to others? Was I looking for sympathy? I wanted to be clear with myself.

In looking for answers, I found some in the unlikeliest of places. For fun one day, I went to see a psychic. I went into the reading with one primary question: "Am I writing this book to help myself or others, and if it is truly for others, why do I feel so guilty about sharing it?" I was staggered by what I heard.

The psychic began by telling me that, when she stepped into my vibration, the first thing she noticed was a fishhook. The hook had me snared, through my skin at my neck/upper back. What the psychic didn't know was that I have had neck and upper back problems for years. I'd been to numerous doctors, massage therapists, acupuncturists and other healers to try and remove what seemed to be a permanent brick that lay just beneath my skin. In fact, my massage therapist often joked with me that I carried a bowling ball on my right shoulder.

As the description continued, I began to cry. It was the first time in my life that I felt as though someone truly understood what I had been feeling for so many years. She continued to say that, although the hook only pierced a few layers of my skin, it was painful. The pain was causing me to not move forward. The line was taut; every time I tried to move forward, I would feel the pain from the hook and stop. What the psychic noted as particularly interesting was how light and thin the line seemed to be, yet how powerful it was at stopping me.

She could have said nothing more and I would have felt as light as air. This was exactly how I'd felt, only described in a way I could never explain. No matter what I had accomplished in my life, or what I wanted to accomplish in my life, it always felt as though something was holding me back. With time, it felt as though the pull grew less and less, but it was there nonetheless.

The question now became, how would I permanently remove that hook and allow myself to be free? In examining my life, I realize that I have been guided to walk along all sorts of paths. Paths that have been thickly lined with trees and brambles. These paths, of course, are the many experiences and choices I have made in the past, choices that I was led to make with the hope of finally freeing myself from the hook.

Ultimately, my path has led me to explore the ideas and lessons in this book. It is this book that has finally allowed me to permanently remove the hook from my shoulder. By addressing and more importantly sharing my story, I have been enabled to continue my journey without pain.

What I have come to accept as the truth is that my mother lived her life in a way that we all wish we could. She answered to no one, and she did what she wanted, when she wanted. There is no doubt that her choices caused pain in the lives of many. But in the end, aren't we all trying to live a life that will bring us joy and happiness? Every choice she made was a choice that she thought would make her happy, bring her peace and joy. No one makes a choice thinking, "I hope this hurts everyone I know." We all make choices that we think will bring happiness. Sometimes we are right, and sometimes we are wrong.

The bottom line is that, if someone told you that you had to move in an hour, you would probably grab a garbage bag and fill it with the things that brought you the most happiness.

CHAPTER NINETEEN
THE REAL COST OF FOSTER CARE

*"All that we are is the result of all
that we have thought."*—Buddha

EARLIER IN THE BOOK, I quoted statistics on where many children who have been in foster care end up in their lives. But if you've made it through the system and are still managing to function in society, you will find that you have lifelong issues that affect you day in and day out. In this chapter, I'll explore these issues.

FOOD

I have a confession to make: I judge people by what they put in their grocery carts. I envision someone's entire life story by what's in his or her grocery cart. I see a correlation, based solely on my own assumptions, between the food they eat and the kind of shape they are in, along with what they are wearing. Then I invent a career, family, and lifestyle based on clues as random as cereal choice, vegetables and fruit, meat, bread, and beverages.

I know other people make judgments based on style of clothes, hairstyle, and the type of car people drive. So I figure that my grocery cart game boils down to my relationship with food, one of the lasting reminders of an abusive childhood.

Every foster child I have met has issues with food. Each may have different issues, handled in many different ways, but we all seem to have them. Mine started before foster care, but after my experiences in care they were reinforced, made a permanent part of who I was.

When your parents, or foster parents, use food as a tool to control you, it's bound to affect how you live daily. My parents used food to punish my brother and me. They starved us if they thought we lied, or broke the rules, or just didn't deserve to eat. And because my parents valued other addictions over food, like drugs and alcohol, grocery shopping was never very high (pun intended) on their to-do list.

Food is a big factor in my life, from not getting enough when I was a child, to worrying about having too much as an adult.

My foster mother made terrible dinners, but her baked goods were delicious. We all gently pushed away the entrées, but devoured her cakes, cookies and pie. I loved sugar as one of the few comforts I got in that house.

When I was out on my own for the first time at college, I had a limited amount of money to buy food, and knew little about how to cook. I don't think I ate any vegetables until college, and even then it was not often. I was unwilling to try new things, preferring to stick with what I knew, like bean burritos from Taco Bell, which used to cost 59 cents and were very filling. I also ate generic boxes of macaroni and cheese. I was brought up not putting milk in mac and cheese, so it tastes strange to me with milk.

The truth: You can't afford to take risks buying something you might not like or don't know how to cook when you're both hungry and broke. I remember going to the grocery store and staring at the meat aisle, wondering how I could possibly cook a pound of ground beef. I had to save up for a pan for months before I got one, and even then it was on layaway.

After I started to have extra spending money, food became a draw. I'd go out to dinner, and suddenly realize I was in a situation where I didn't have to order the cheapest thing on the menu. I could get a lot. I wanted a lot. It all seemed so appealing, so appetizing. I wanted to know that I could have it just because I could. I had money, and I could spend it on food and myself.

When Gerry and I had enough space and cash, I started stocking food to the point of hoarding. While I know the Red Cross advises to stock enough provisions for a few days without power during a blizzard or hurricane, I had enough to last us for an entire winter of blizzards. Apocalypse coming? No problem. Now, if I find I don't have enough canned goods, I have a panic attack. Yet perhaps Sophia has raided them for a food drive for the local rescue mission. I have a visceral need to see that my family is not in any danger of starving, at least for a few weeks or months.

Along with the ability to hoard food and eat whatever I wanted off the menu came a slow but steady weight gain. I went from skin and bones to obese, according to my body mass index. Last year, I decided that I was going to lose the weight. I was the heaviest I had ever been, and with my new-found freedom at work, it seemed that my weight was the next thing I needed to conquer. I started with steady exercise, counting my steps with a pedometer. Once I was walking five miles a day, I added a daily yoga class, sometimes more than one fitness class a day. I started to count my calories. With all that effort, I lost nearly forty pounds.

And then I stopped losing weight. I was eating very little food, exercising like crazy, but I stopped losing. It was maddening. I had a goal weight in mind, and I had stopped making progress in zeroing in on that number. I hovered at the same weight for eight weeks, gradually becoming more and more obsessive, logging my food intake.

So I went to see a nutritionist for help. She took down all the information about my diet and exercise plan, and concluded that I was not eating enough food. I had taken too many calories off my meal plan, and it was not healthy. She developed a whole menu plan that was sensible and nutritious, including all the foods I already eat, and some of my favorites. She did a fabulous job, but I couldn't follow the plan. Not even for a day. I rationalized before even getting to my car in the parking lot of her office that it was too much food, and there was no way I could eat it all.

Control and punishment. In a way, I'm punishing myself for not losing more weight by withholding food, just as my parents punished me. Punishment must follow failure. I know it's stupid, but...

It's a constant push and pull. I really love food, and want to try new food and experiment with food. I feel loss of control now even if I eat one cheese cracker, because I know if I eat one, then I'll eat the whole box. Old habits kick in, and I think I need to eat as much as I can now, lest I be denied dinner. I don't know how to fix that mixed-up file in my brain. This is one of the many life-long effects of childhood abuse and neglect, one of those little things that make you feel that you don't belong in society as an adult.

When I speak with foster families, they all seem concerned about food issues. Often I hear examples of how their kids will only eat a very specific regimen. For instance, one little boy only ate peanut butter and jelly sandwiches. I try to offer some context to the problem, and give examples from my own life along some common-sense advice to try and help out these families. But in the end, food is heavily linked to psychological issues. How privation affects children, especially those in foster care, needs to be studied further.

MONEY
When you grew up like I did — hungry, wearing cast-off clothes, living in housing where the scarce furniture was battered and worn out — it's hard to ever feel comfortable and relaxed where money is concerned. That is especially true when you and your husband own your own business. There's no regular salary, no paid vacations, no benefits, and always a fear that one day the work will stop coming in, leaving you unable to pay bills. I don't know if I'll ever feel like we have enough money.

When you grow up in poverty, you learn bad financial behaviors that stick with you forever. Unlearning these behaviors is difficult. Like all things, sometimes the only way you can change is to understand the hard way that what your parents did wasn't necessarily the right thing.

One of the things I learned growing up was that all extra money had to be spent immediately. I remember listening to my mother's conversations with my stepdad, friends or family, most of them surrounding the topic of money. There was never enough. Nobody had any. It seemed as elusive as the hidden treasure of Atlantis. If you had any money, then the next thing you had to do was spend the money. There were always things that needed to be paid, including rent, utilities, food, and car insurance. There were heated debates about which ones really needed to be paid that week, and which ones could wait a few more days. These decisions would often leave us cold, hungry, or both. You can never have too much money, and as soon as you have it, spend it, or you might lose it.

This is a terrible habit, and makes no long-term sense. But when you are used to having nothing, allowing yourself to have money in a savings account feels like a luxury.

Another lasting effect of growing up poor is the need to go overboard on gift-giving. This is a constant struggle for me, and has been for a number of years. It's not hard to understand if you read about my life as a child. Needless to say, I received very few gifts. Birthday and holidays were often forgotten. On the rare occasion that I might receive a gift from a friend, I was often asked to return it, so that my parents could use the money to pay bills. Once I started to have success in my career and I wanted to buy my husband as many gifts as possible. I loved to spoil him. I remember one Christmas clearly as it took him nearly two days to open all of his gifts. I knew that I had gone overboard, but I couldn't help myself. I still struggle with not spoiling Gerry and Sophia.

On the other hand, I'm a very bad gift receiver. It's awkward for me if I have to open a present in front of the person giving the gift. "These are great," I say, but people don't feel that I am really enjoying their thoughtfulness. Perhaps this comes from not being practiced in receiving gifts, or from not seeing myself as deserving, I'm not sure. But I do know that I'm not alone in my difficulty. It's shared by millions of foster care survivors.

PEOPLE SKILLS

For me, one of the major lifelong effects of growing up in a dysfunctional, neglectful, abusive home, and then going into foster care, is that it's really hard for me to like and trust other people. We moved so often as a child it was difficult for me to ever have a long-term friendship. By the time I got into a more stable situation in my foster care home, the damage had already been done: I was so wary of being myself and telling the truth about my family situation that I could never engage in deep conversations, make strong opinions, or be the life of the party. I didn't trust that people liked the person I was, because I knew I wasn't being myself.

My gut reaction is to believe most people are lying all of the time, or that they want something. I live in a state of perpetual doubt and angst over where I stand in any relationship. I also have a difficult time asking people for favors. I don't mind doing things for others. I will go out of my way to help, but it's difficult for me to ask for the same assistance. I assume I'll be let down. I am positive these interpersonal problems all stem from my childhood, growing up in utter chaos and dysfunction. I fear that, if somebody is being nice to me, she or he must have an agenda. My first instinct is to ask, "What do they want from me, really?"

It probably doesn't help that, in the process of running a law office, Gerry and I are exposed to all of the town secrets and misdeeds. We hear about the divorces, the cheating, the drug use, the stealing, and the cons. This makes me cynical about whether anybody is truly on the up and up.

I've always wanted to be liked, but I'm starting to care less about what other people think about me. Maybe it's because of the life experiences I've had and the people I've met, but now I just assume people don't like me. I don't usually banter wittily or engage in superficial conversations, so people might think I'm cold and unfriendly. It's hard for me now to lie or put on a front.

My world-view is heavily influenced by the fact that I lived for a considerable period without reliable food or housing, and that the people I should have been able to trust the most in the world abandoned me. Conversations about what people did over the weekend or what TV show they're into don't engage me. Instead, I worry daily about people who are involved in real-life disasters, like our dysfunctional foster care system. I'm not saying that those light conversation starters are a bad thing, I just have a hard time joining in. Perhaps I never learned how.

While people have recommended therapy to relieve myself of the anxiety and stress, I can't accept that it would actually help, and don't see how it could aid me to move forward. I don't have trust in the process of therapy, specifically because it requires a relationship based on trust. And truthfully, after being forced into counseling as a teenager, when I was diagnosed with various misleading disorders, this lack of trust has stayed with me.

So for me, continuing my education through classes and educational forums, as well as reading, travel, meeting new people, and sharing stories about foster care, helps me to heal. I try to put into practice the things I have read about positivity, forgiveness, and the law of attraction in a meaningful and purposeful way. The first step in changing my life and taking control was learning forgiveness of both myself and those that I held so much anger for in my life, especially those whom I felt had abandoned me. Learning forgiveness has given me the nourishment that I needed to create my life on my terms.

CHAPTER TWENTY
WHERE THE RUBBER MEETS THE ROAD

"When it comes to getting things done, we need fewer architects and more bricklayers." —Colleen Barrett

FOSTER CARE HAS BECOME an accepted necessity in our society. But, like prisons and the welfare system, most Americans believe that the foster care system is something we can't fix. It's just a necessary evil of living in a nation as large as ours, with parents who can't fulfill their obligations to raise their own children.

The statistics support the reality of foster care. There are about 400,000 children in foster care on any given day in the United States, equivalent to the populations of Atlanta, Georgia or Washington D.C. Some kids are in for a short-term stay, and others until they "age out,[6]" but regardless of how long they stay, the numbers continue to grow each year. The federal government and most states don't keep statistics on kids after they leave the system, but what we do know is the following.

- About 61% age out without having a place to live, either with a family or their own place, rendering them homeless.
- Less than 3% will go to college, less than 1% will receive a degree.
- Less than 50% have received a high school diploma or G.E.D.
- Over 50% are unemployed, and over 80% will become a parent and receive some form of public assistance within two years of aging out.

---

6   Aging out refers to the age a child reaches before the system is no longer required to keep track of the child. This age varies by state.

Foster children are also given psychotropic medications 12 times as frequently as other low-income children living with their biological families. The Casey Family study showed they experience Post Traumatic Stress Disorder (PTSD) at twice the rate of Iraqi war veterans. Despite their increased need for health services, nearly 33 percent of adult foster care alumni surveyed had no health insurance. Adults who had been in foster care as children suffered worse prognoses than their peers in almost all domains. This chart contrasts those who were in foster care to the general population.

AILMENT	FOSTER CARE	GENERAL POP
PTSD	25%	4.5%
DEPRESSION	24.3%	10.6%
ANXIETY	43%	5.1%
ADDICTION	11.1%	2.5%
MALES CONVICTED OF A CRIME	60%	10%
HOMELESS FOR MORE THAN A DAY	22%	2%

It sounds bad, and it is. Amarillo, Texas reported that it had 349 children in care. Of those, it was estimated that 40% to 50% would never complete high school. 66% would become homeless, go to jail or die within one year of leaving the system. If those odds weren't difficult enough, National Statistics predicted that out of the about

1,613,803 inmates housed in federal and state prisons in 2006, over 80% had been in foster care at some point in their lives. That's 1,291,042 inmates who had been in foster care.

The United States federal, state and local governments spent nearly $23 billion on child welfare systems in 2006. That seems like a big number: About $57,500 in spending per child that year. However, in the same year the federal, state and local governments spent over $78 billion on incarcerated inmates. So the question is: Why are we willing to spend money on our children after they are convicted of a crime, but not before?

The simple truth is that we are failing our children in foster care. Comic Monroe Martin grew up in foster care and describes it well. As I recently heard him relate, in foster care authorities step in when they suspect abuse and neglect and remove children from their homes. They then place them in new homes with the same circumstances, except surrounded by strangers.

Statistics vary, but some say as many as two out of five children placed in foster homes are abused or neglected. So what's the best answer beyond foster care? Orphanages? Residential Treatment Facilities? I have been pondering this question for years.

I am adamant that new solutions need to be implemented. For me, the reason is clear: I can't stand by and watch more and more children left to suffer on their own, without support and guidance. I know that most individuals will never truly understand those sensations of utter loneliness, the things you feel when you can't be loved by your own parent. However, what these individuals tend to overlook is how foster children are a part of their communities, and often are a source for many of the community resources and funds, not only as children but as adults. That includes more jails, longer times on unemployment, teen and unplanned pregnancies, homelessness.

Where do prisoners come from? Where do teen mothers come from? What characteristics do they have in common? And how can we prevent the causes at the start? For me these are very real and brutal questions.

The outcomes of foster care are real. We know that foster children go to prison and have criminal records at much higher rates than their peers. Yet, we do nothing. We know that girls in foster care are more likely to become pregnant before graduating high school than their contemporaries, yet there is little being done. We know that foster youth experience unemployment and homelessness at much higher rates, and again, nothing is being done.

This is not just an issue of addressing a broken system for a few children, but rather understanding the effects the broken system has on children, resulting in adults that can't function in a world that has warehoused them, giving them an incarcerated mentality.

We can all agree that foster homes sometimes work. Orphanages sometimes work. But statistically speaking, the numbers are weak. We create a population of adults and children who have never experienced non-abusive behaviors, and then wonder why they can't comply with the accepted norms of society. News flash: The accepted norms we have taught them are violence, lack of empathy, and to watch out for themselves first, taking from the system every chance they can.

Foster care means having social workers watching for kids to make mistakes. What may be deemed normal childhood behavior in a regular family suddenly falls under the scope of troubled once a child is in foster care. A school, on the other hand, diminishes children's access to bad behavior in both the foster home and their biological parent's home.

Most foster care alumni I speak with say that they don't mention their time in foster care to other people, mostly because people who've never been in the system just don't understand. I know I didn't want to mention that I'd been in foster care. I believed people would discriminate against me as a result. But with nearly 400,000 kids in care each year, how can we continue on this path? We need more foster care alums to stand up and offer their voices and willingness to help.

Here are some of my proposed solutions:

ALTERNATIVE #1: BOARDING SCHOOLS

In order to understand what we can do to fix this badly damaged system, I had to look to the past. In doing so, I found an unlikely guide: a man who was not well educated himself, making it only to the fifth grade, who eventually struck it big in the chocolate business. Milton Hershey was unable to have children of his own, and he and his wife founded the Hershey Industrial School for Boys in Pennsylvania in 1909. The first class started with ten students, and today the institution serves almost 2,000 students per year. Milton Hershey School is a cost-free, private, coeducational home and school for children from families of low income, limited resources, and social need. It is also a prime example of how we can solve our foster care crisis around the country.

I have never been one to complain about a system without having a possible solution. For many years, not having a solution was the main reason I didn't want to discuss my time in care. Sure, I could share the stories about what happened, the scars that it left on my life, but I didn't know what else could be done to fix it in a broader sense. Then one day, I heard the words "What if you did the opposite?" while listening to a podcast with lifestyle author Tim Ferriss.

It got me thinking. What was the opposite of all these terrible statistics? Where were the kids with the above 90% graduation rate? What was a common denominator among the most successful people in the United States? I started researching. According to a study conducted by the Arts & Science Group of Baltimore on behalf of the Association of Boarding Schools:

- Boarding school students are more likely to achieve positions of management earlier in their careers than their peers at private day or public schools, and reach higher management positions throughout their careers.

- Boarding school students are much less likely to watch television or play video games than their peers, from high school into adulthood.
- Boarding school students are also more philanthropic as adults, continuing a pervasive tradition of service.

The study also dispels stereotypes that persist in popular culture about boarding schools as havens for rich and troubled children:

- Boarding school students are not sent away, but rather choose to enroll primarily because of the high quality academics.
- Boarding schools are not homogeneous.
- Most boarding school students said their social lives do not revolve around drugs and alcohol.
- About 70% of boarders said that school helped them develop self-discipline, maturity, independence and the ability to think critically.
- About 87% of boarding school graduates reported being very well prepared academically for college, compared to 71% of private day and 39% of public school alumni.

So what if a boarding school for some foster students was opened as an alternative to traditional placements? It has plenty of initial positives:

- Removing children physically from locations that may be abusive.
- Providing not only stability and security, but also consistency, which seem to be lacking in almost every foster child's life.
- Providing housing and potentially transitional housing for those students who graduate and move on to college, but have no place to live during college breaks including holidays and summers.
- Providing mentors, teachers and other students who understand the specific needs and challenges that only foster children experience.

- The ability for foster children to be treated as children who can accomplish great things, rather than children who we pray don't end up like their parents.

Note: The idea of a boarding school for foster youth should not be confused with orphanages, residential treatment facilities, or group homes. I believe that to truly be successful, the priority is on being a school. Think Harry Potter. In addition to putting all the foster kids on an even playing field socially, like any school, there will naturally be great students and students who struggle. Perhaps most important is that this school offers a safe and stable environment for children to live in. I believe the ideals of security and education can turn around our failing system.

A boarding school allows children to invest time in their futures, rather than waste time explaining their pasts.

The miraculous thing is, this boarding school model already exists, and has been succeeding for nearly two decades. The Crossnore School, located in Crossnore, North Carolina, has been performing miracles for children in that region for over 100 years, but has been specifically using their current model for the past 15 years.

The Crossnore School accepts children ages 1-21, and is on 85 acres in the picturesque Blue Ridge Mountains. School leaders offer a holistic approach to treating the whole child emotionally, physically, mentally and spiritually, using their Theory of Change Model[7] as well as modalities based upon the Adverse Childhood Experiences model.[8]

---

7   Theory of Change is a specific type of methodology for planning, participation and evaluation that is used in the philanthropy, not-for-profit and government sectors to promote social change.

8   Adverse Childhood Experience (or ACE's) describes a traumatic experience in a person's life occurring before the age of 18 that a person remembers as an adult. Individuals are given an ACE's score based on nine (9) possible life events, including physical abuse, sexual abuse, emotional abuse, mental illness of a household member, drinking or alcoholism in the home, prescription or street drug abuse in the home, divorce or separation, domestic violence toward a parent, or incarceration of a parent.

What is unique about the Crossnore School it is a residential foster care group with a public K-12 Charter School which all of the children attend along other children from the community. Crossnore is uniquely different in that it accepts placement from State Agencies as well as private placements. This hybrid model offers the best of all circumstances.

Currently the Crossnore School serves 80 children, with a lengthy waiting list. This is an organization that can boast an over 90% graduation rate, with nearly all graduates going on to college. It is hard to find any school with those kinds of statistics. Yet, every day the school leaders are fighting to find and keep funding.

When I spoke to the current CEO, Brett Loftis, he said, "We have created a unique model of care comprised of holistic health care and spiritual development, comprehensive life enrichments skills, coordinated case management and advocacy, research-based therapeutic services, and rigorous education. But at its core, Crossnore is a safe, loving home where children come to heal."

ALTERNATIVE #2: FOSTERING THE WHOLE FAMILY

Another idea that could be considered, either on its own or in conjunction with a boarding school, is the concept of fostering the whole family. There has been much discussion on the trauma a child experiences when physically removed from home and placed in care. Additionally, statistics show that of the almost 400,000 children in foster care, half have a case goal of reunification with their biological families.

Fostering the whole family is a new concept that is currently being tested in a program in St. Paul, Minnesota. There, the county's social service department gives the option for the whole family to be placed in foster care. The target group is adult parents and minor children without stable residences, where the children are at risk of placement in out-of-home care. Although the parents and children may have special needs, there are no safety risks that would necessitate separating children and parents.

This is one area that needs exploring, the application can be made in other areas as well. The rate of recidivism of the children of those who were in foster care themselves is remarkable, estimated at between 80% to 92%. It makes sense. If you didn't have a good role model of a parent when you were growing up, it's hard to know how to act when you become a parent yourself. Perhaps by fostering both parents and children together, we could better address the needs of our communities. There are numerous stories of children being placed within foster homes, sometimes even being adopted, only for the foster or adoptive parent to receive a call asking if they would be interested in taking another child recently born to the same mother. This is a call that can happen three, four, or even five times. In part this occurs because the needs and challenges of the birth mother have never been properly addressed. This is the obvious root cause of the need for care in the first place.

By fostering the whole family, we have a chance to show how to make better decisions, and hopefully to help prevent future unwanted pregnancies, especially when the birth mother has addiction issues that need to be addressed.

HIDDEN STATISTICS OF FOSTER CARE

Most foster care alumni classify themselves as independent and resilient. They acknowledge that they look out for themselves before anyone or anything else. Additionally, I began interviewing foster care alumni who consider themselves successful in adult life, and all have at least a bachelor's degree or higher. When I began talking to these alumni, I realized how much we all have in common. All:

- Credit a specific teacher or education as the reason for their success.
- Felt marginalized as children, and say they are not sure they will ever feel satisfied with their accomplishments.

- Believe that they are great gift givers and givers in general. Most would give their last penny when asked. However, all believe they are the worst gift receivers. Most acknowledge that during their time in care, their birthdays were often empty, and that the holidays could be a confusing time.
- Are loners. With the exception of spouses and children, most of the former alumni I spoke to classified themselves as loners. Those who did not said they kept friends at a distance, and didn't believe they had a best friend.
- Are independent. Most were not allowed to attend camps, participate in sports and activities because of the cost. Those who were allowed to do these things had to figure it out on their own, including all costs and transportation.

One former foster child said she received a tremendous amount of help from a school guidance counselor when applying for college scholarships. She received a full ride. However, when in college she still needed a place to live on holidays and breaks. Her former foster family told her she could come back, but that she had to pay full room and board. This is another problem area that I believe the boarding school could be successful in helping. We could allow our students to come back and live in the dorms on campus during these down times at college, again providing a safe and secure place. That is especially needed during the holidays, which tend to be very difficult for most youth.

It is clear that the current foster care system has been largely unsuccessful in transitioning youth who are in the system to becoming productive, independent adults. Study after study cites the atrocious statistics. We can no longer allow our youth to decay within a system that has become a holding tank for the criminal justice system, the welfare system, and various other forms of public assistance.

What is needed are long-term placements for these children, placements that last until adulthood. We must look to well-run facilities that provide stable environments over time, educational opportunities, and the chance for children to develop emotionally in secure and nurturing environments, such as those found at Crossnore, the Hershey School, and Boys Town in Nebraska.

We owe it to our most vulnerable citizens, our children, to take a chance, drop our fears and move forward with love, forgiveness and a commitment to make a change. Together we must focus on solutions and move forward into greatness!

AUTHOR'S NOTE

The cause is real. There are over 400,000 foster children each day in the United States alone, and the number is growing rapidly. Each year over 24,000 children will age out of the system. When they do, most will become homeless and unemployed; many will develop a criminal record. They deserve more. If you are interested in learning ways in which you can get involved, along with me, to reform the foster care system, please contact me or join my newsletter at www.garbagebagsuitcase.com or check out the resources section of this book. None of us can change the past. But, together we can focus on solutions and start taking action on the positive changes we all agree need to happen.

ACKNOWLEDGMENTS

When I initially set out to tell this story, I thought it was a crazy endeavor that I wasn't sure I could return from or even finish. The truth is, I wouldn't have started nor finished without the help, inspiration, reminders, critiques, criticism, encouragement and love of a lot of individuals.

My husband has an unwavering belief in me. No matter how many times I try to talk him out of it, he never relents. Without his steadfast confidence in my ability to write this book and to carry on the mission, I too would be a statistic left on a page. He kept his belief in me during many times of reading the manuscript, editing, and even listening to me rant about the process.

A great many thanks goes to my daughter, who has enough confidence for the both of us. She never allowed me to give up, even in my darkest times and even when she couldn't utter a word. During this process, her quick wit, sarcasm, keen eye for detail and humor kept me moving forward and reminded me that having her in my life is the greatest honor I could ever receive.

My sincere and deepest gratitude to the many, many people who saw me through this book and its various stages and incarnations; to those who provided support, talked things over, read, wrote, offered comments, assisted in editing, proofreading, design and all else. I thank you Jeff Peek, Nicole Bagi, Betsy Thorpe, John Robert Williams, Caroline Noonan, Zeke Fleet, Joe Wilkinson, Paula McLain, Allison Risoli, Carolyn Risoli, Susie Greenfelder, Ed Ketterer, The Mission Point Press Team: Anne Stanton, Doug Weaver, Scott Courterier, Heather Shaw, Jennifer Carroll, and my JKS Communications Team: Julie Schoerke and Marissa Curnutte.

A special thanks goes to my father, who understands that telling this story is not about reliving the past and pointing fingers. But it is about changing the lives of the children who currently feel unloved and unwanted. To change things for them we still have a chance to make a difference.

I also owe a huge thank you to a long list of agents and assistants who looked over my proposal and sample chapters. They all said no, but some gave me great feedback and insight that allowed me to make this book into what it has become. I am forever indebted.

Last, but not least, a thank you to everyone whom I have not listed by name, but who inspired this book, listened to me complain and helped me heal from within.

RESOURCES

While research and writing this book I have come across many resources and experts, from various fields, that reflect the notion of moving our attention to solutions to our pressing social crisis issues and taking action for change. Many have spent lifetimes researching these topics. Without their dedication I would not have been able to not only heal myself, but I would not have been able to understand the depths in which trauma can affect us all.

If you are interested in learning more about any of the topics discussed in my book, then I highly suggest you look to some of these wonderful resources:

BOOKS, ARTICLES AND STUDIES

The Adverse Childhood Experiences (ACE) Study. Centers for Disease Control and Prevention, via their website www.cdc.g.

J.S. Middlebrooks and Natalie Audage. *The Effects of Childhood Stress on Health Across the Lifespan.* Centers for Disease Control. (2008)

Rebecca Ruiz. *How Childhood Trauma Could Be Mistaken for ADHD*, The Atlantic Magazine. (July 2014)

Donna Jackson Nakazawa. *Childhood Disrupted,* Atria Books. (2015)

Christian Moore. *The Resilience Breakthrough: 27 tools for turning Adversity into Action,* Self Published. (2014)

WEBSITES

Dr. Vincent Felitti, M.D. at http://www.acestudy.org/speakers/
vincent_j_felitti_md

Aces too High at http://acestoohigh.com
ACE's Connection at http://www.acesconnection.com

The Sanctuary Model at http://www.sanctuaryweb.com

The Theory of Change Model at http://www.theoryofchange.
org

The Crossnore School at www.thecrossnoreschool.org

The Hershey School at http://www.mhskids.org

Safe to Learn at http://www.safetolearn.com

Open Table at http://www.theopentable.org

Substance Abuse and Mental Services Administration at
http://www.samhsa.gov

Cure Violence at http://cureviolence.or

PLEASE TAKE A MOMENT to ask yourself the following questions formed from the study. It was coordinated by The Centers for Disease Control and Prevention and Kaiser Permanente's Health Appraisal Clinic.

Prior to your eighteenth birthday:

- Did a parent or another adult in the household often or very often...swear at you, insult you, put you down or humiliate you? Or act in a way that made you afraid that you might be physically hurt?
- Did a parent or another adult in the household often or very often...push, grab, slap, or throw something at you? Or ever hit you so hard that you had marks or were injured?
- Did an adult or person at least five years older than you ever touch or fondle you or have you touch their body in a sexual way? Or attempt to touch you or touch you inappropriately or sexually abuse you?
- Did you often or very often feel that...no one in your family loved you or thought you were important or special? Or feel that your family members didn't look out for one another, feel close to one another, or support one another?
- Did you often or very often feel that...you didn't have enough to eat, had to wear dirty clothes, and had no one to protect you? Or that your parents were too drunk or high on drugs to take care of you or take you to the doctor if needed?
- Was a biological parent ever lost to you through divorce, abandonment or another reason?
- Was your mother or stepmother often or ever often pushed, grabbed, slapped, or was an object thrown at her? Or was she sometimes, often or ever often kicked, bitten, hit with a fist or hit with something hard? Or was she ever repeatedly hit over

the course of at least a few minutes or threatened with a gun or knife?

- Did you live with anyone who was a problem drinker or alcoholic, or who used street drugs?
- Was a household member depressed or mentally ill, or did a household member attempt suicide?
- Did a household member go to prison?

After you have answered these questions, it may be easier to see how your (or your loved ones) experiences are affecting your physical, emotional and mental well-being. As you think of your own experiences, or the experiences of those in your community, these questions may better help you understand why some people have reactions to situations that you might not otherwise understand. When we stop asking, "What is wrong with that person?" and instead start asking, "What has happened to that person?" We can begin to change outcomes for those who have suffered great losses.